UNLEASHING STUDENT
SUPERPOWERS

UNLEASHING STUDENT

Practical Teaching Strategies for 21st Century Students

SUPERPOWERS

KRISTEN SWANSON

HADLEY J. FERGUSON

FOREWORD BY MARILEE SPRENGER

CORWIN
A SAGE Company

CORWIN
A SAGE Company

FOR INFORMATION:

Corwin

A SAGE Company

2455 Teller Road

Thousand Oaks, California 91320

(800) 233-9936

www.corwin.com

SAGE Publications Ltd.

1 Oliver's Yard

55 City Road

London EC1Y 1SP

United Kingdom

SAGE Publications India Pvt. Ltd.

B 1/I 1 Mohan Cooperative Industrial Area

Mathura Road, New Delhi 110 044

India

SAGE Publications Asia-Pacific Pte. Ltd.

3 Church Street

#10-04 Samsung Hub

Singapore 049483

Acquisitions Editor: Robin Najar

Associate Editor: Desirée A. Bartlett

Editorial Assistant: Ariel Price

Production Editor: Melanie Birdsall

Copy Editor: Lana Todorovic-Arndt

Typesetter: C&M Digitals (P) Ltd.

Proofreader: Theresa Kay

Indexer: Sheila Bodell

Cover and Interior Designer: Janet Kiesel

Printed in the United States of America

Library of Congress Cataloging-in-Publication Data

Swanson, Kristen.

Unleashing student superpowers : practical teaching strategies for 21st century students / Kristen Swanson, Hadley J. Ferguson.

pages cm
Includes bibliographical references and index.

ISBN 978-1-4833-5096-7 (pbk.)

1. Teaching—Methodology. 2. Active learning. I. Ferguson, Hadley J. II. Title.

LB1025.3.S93 2014
371.102—dc23   2013051250

This book is printed on acid-free paper.

SUSTAINABLE FORESTRY INITIATIVE
Certified Chain of Custody
Promoting Sustainable Forestry
www.sfiprogram.org
SFI-01268
SFI label applies to text stock

14 15 16 17 18 10 9 8 7 6 5 4 3 2 1

CONTENTS

4. THE CURATING INSTRUCTIONAL JOURNEY: SOLVING A PUZZLE

FOREWORD

I spend most of my time providing professional development to teachers about applying brain research in the classroom, using differentiated instructional strategies, and how to use the Common Core State Standards and prepare for their assessments. When Kristen Swanson and Hadley Ferguson asked me to write this foreword, I took my time reading the manuscript and researching their work. I wanted to be certain that they were offering information that would fit the needs of a diverse population of teachers who were certainly facing the most diverse classrooms they had ever encountered. I know that teachers struggle with engagement, rigor, motivation, and technology. I was hopeful that this book would be among those that offered practical strategies to increase all of these. I was not disappointed.

We have learned through brain research that the person doing the most talking is doing the most learning. In the past, the talker has always been the teacher, trying hard to do a good job and thus providing information for students to absorb and apply. In the present, teachers are asking probing, critical questions to stimulate higher-level thinking. Students, however, have not previously been taught how to think critically or creatively. They were also used to giving only the one "right" answer, so they were often reluctant to participate. Teachers are trying to make changes to meet new standards, adding technology to their curriculum, and feeling some pressure from new teacher-evaluation systems. Many feel challenged or even overwhelmed as they tackle the new more rigorous standards as well as performing at a distinguished level in their chosen profession. In the future, the ideas in a book such as this one will lead us to the necessary changes with ease and with positive results! But the future is now.

It is time we not only engage learners, but also empower them. In order for this to occur, teachers must be empowered first. *Unleashing Student Superpowers: Practical Teaching Strategies for 21st Century Students* will take you on an instructional journey that will give you the control to step back and let the power within your students shine through. This is a guide that encompasses the most important processes to provide total engagement, encourage questioning and research, think outside the box to create and synthesize, and embed formative assessment throughout the journey.

Swanson and Ferguson provide the bricks for the road you can follow and offer you plans for success for both you and your students. *Unleashing Student Superpowers* provides differentiation strategies, rubrics, real classroom scenarios, standard connections, learning activities, and technology ideas and upgrades. The authors have done the legwork to offer teachers an approach not only to student-centered classrooms, but to student-led classrooms. If you are involved in teacher evaluation, you know that a student-led classroom with students asking the questions is a hallmark of a distinguished teacher.

If you have been running from technology, run no more. This resource provides websites to appeal to the most digital student brains as well as to those of us who find technology challenging, and the authors also supply tools that will deliver the same outcomes that are not technology-based. This is a win-win for students, teachers, and administrators. The technology suggested includes mostly free, easy-to-access, and useful sites that will excite your students and help lead them to mastery. All of the lesson resources are found on Pinterest, where students are introduced to the superpowers and find activities to assist in understanding those powers and using them.

Unleashing Student Superpowers will make heroes out of teachers and students. As you revisit and refine your teaching practices, you will see motivated, engaged, and happy students. The plans for journeying through questioning, gaming, curating, designing, digital inking, and connecting are presented in such a way to make you feel more confident about teaching the 21st century student. You will be giving students the opportunity to be superheroes in their own minds, and you will certainly be a superhero to them as they learn how to approach school as a place to engage their minds, expand their thinking, and become leaders for their learning.

Collaboration is apparent throughout the book. The idea that two heads are better than one is apparent in this publication. These writers have created a book that is smoothly written, well organized, and full of great ideas. For those educators looking for ways to create a safe and exciting learning environment, this book is for you. For those educators who need some help with technology, this book is for you. And for those educators who are curious about what superpowers can be unleashed in your students, this book will provide information, instructions, and examples that will change the way you view your students and your role in their futures.

—Marilee Sprenger
Adjunct Professor
Aurora University, IL

A PREFACE FROM THE SUPERPOWER GUARDIANS

Do you sometimes wish that you could whip on a flowing cape and pick up a magic wand? That you could wave it once over your classroom full of students and have them become masters of all that they need to know?

We're teachers just like you, and we know that teaching is a difficult, yet rewarding, profession. The biggest "wins" come when we can see our students grow and develop as independent, engaged learners. We've developed this text to provide you with practical changes that help you cultivate *learning superpowers* in all of your students.

With careful instructional design, students can hone the superpowers necessary to master whatever they encounter! It is our job as teachers to create classrooms and learning experiences that empower struggling students who aren't good at the game of school, especially those who lose confidence under the pressure of grading and testing. How many talented learners have been labeled by their faults instead of their strengths?

While we cannot solve all of the problems that exist outside of our classrooms, we can provide a safe haven within which they can learn while they are with us. We can establish classroom rules that forbid criticism and social abuse. We can encourage and empower with every word that we speak. It is only for the hours of school, but it can encourage growth and learning in deep and fundamental ways.

Like the X-Men, Superman, and all other superheroes, each of our students needs to develop his or her talents in unique and original ways. No two students will have the same combination of powers or strategies. Each is a unique individual with powers that grow from within him or her. This individuality is not only preferable; it's wonderfully exciting.

The purpose of this book is to empower YOU, the teacher, to unleash the powers within your students, so that they can tackle 21st century challenges, by providing you with practical ideas and resources.

Look for our super tips and comments throughout the book. Anywhere you see our wand, you'll know that we're showing you something extra important.

In addition, we have set up a website at **www.studentsuperpowers.com** and a Pinterest account at **http://pinterest.com/ssuperpowers/boards** where you can access all of the resources in the book. Be sure to follow us on Twitter as well for updates and extra offerings!

These are items, tasks, or ideas that have worked especially well in our classrooms and in classrooms across the nation. We're here to guide you and learn with you every step of the way!

—Kristen (@kristenswanson) and Hadley (@hadleyjf)

ACKNOWLEDGMENTS

This book would not exist without the constant support of my family, friends, and personal learning network. I am grateful to everyone who has given their time, consideration, and ideas to this work.

Countless classroom teachers have shaped this book, by either generously opening their classrooms or prodding my thinking via social media. Specifically, my coauthor Hadley has strengthened my writing and refined my thinking about world class instruction for kids.

Finally, I would like to thank my husband, family, and friends for supporting me and my commitment to the education profession.

—Kristen Swanson

This book is the product of a journey, one that could never have been done alone. I am grateful to all of the teachers with whom I have worked over the years who have helped me learn and grow as an educator. They tirelessly listened and advised as I tested new ideas and wrestled with different ways of helping students grow. I am grateful also that I teach in a school where new ideas are encouraged.

Writing this book provided Kristen and me with a chance to live out a credo in which we both believe, that educators are better together than in isolation. Her questions and encouragement have made me a better teacher and writer!

Most of all, I have to thank all of my family, especially my husband and four children for all of the love, support, and laughter through the years. I can't imagine taking this journey without them!

—Hadley J. Ferguson

PUBLISHER'S ACKNOWLEDGMENTS

Corwin gratefully acknowledges the following peer reviewers for their editorial insight and guidance:

Nancy Foote, National Board Certified Teacher
Higley Unified School District
Gilbert, AZ

Dr. Rebecca L. Mann, Professor
Hope College
Holland, MI

Robin Stewart, Principal
Rolling Hills Elementary School
Fairfield, CA

Deborah D. Therriault, High School Special Education Teacher
Clarkston Community Schools
Clarkston, MI

Kelly Ussery, Teacher
Pleasant Knoll Elementary
Fort Mill, SC

Robert Whallon, Research Assistant
University of Illinois at Urbana-Champaign
Champaign, IL

Dr. Cynthia L. Wilson, Associate Professor
Chair of the Department of Teacher Education
University of Illinois
Springfield, IL

ABOUT THE AUTHORS

Kristen Swanson, EdD, helps teachers design meaningful, interactive curricula at the local and national level. She has taught at the elementary level, served as a regional consultant for Response to Intervention, and worked as an educational technology director for a public school district in Pennsylvania. She holds a BA degree from DeSales University, two MA degrees from Wilkes University, and an EdD degree from Widener University. Kristen is currently an adjunct in the DeSales University instructional technology MEd program and a senior research leader for BrightBytes.

In addition to her experience as an educator, Kristen is also passionate about meaningful professional learning. She serves on the board of the Edcamp Foundation, a nonprofit organization designed to facilitate local, grassroots professional development. She has shared her ideas and expertise at ASCD conferences, TEDxPhiladelphiaEd, TEDxNYED, and Educon. She has also been published in academic journals, including *Literacy Learning: The Middle Years* and the *Journal of Reading, Writing, and Literacy.* She is the author of *Professional Learning in the Digital Age: The Educator's Guide to User-Generated Learning* and *Teaching the Common Core Speaking and Listening Standards.*

Kristen is active in the educational technology sphere. She is a Google Certified Teacher, Twitter Teacher, Edublog Award Nominee, and avid blogger. She strongly believes that rigorous curriculum fosters meaningful technology integration, and she is also interested in the learning opportunities provided by asynchronous learning.

Hadley J. Ferguson is a middle school teacher at Springside Chestnut Hill Academy, an independent school in Philadelphia. She teaches history and humanities as well as entrepreneurship. Hadley is passionate about developing new curriculum to meet the needs of her students, working with other teachers, both in her building and through her personal learning network, to develop the best strategies to enhance the learning in her classroom. Hadley has a BA and an MEd from Smith College.

Because of her experiences of how important collaboration is for learning and growing as an educator, Hadley is actively involved in helping to develop connections among educators. She is a member of the Library of Congress' Teaching with Primary Sources Mentor Advisory group, where she helps teachers connect with the Library. She also advises groups of teachers on strategies for working together to develop curriculum that includes the resources from the Library of Congress. She was named a "Teacher of the Future" by the National Association of Independent Schools and part of a network to enhance support for independent school teachers. Hadley also serves on the board of the Edcamp Foundation, a nonprofit organization designed to facilitate local, grassroots professional development.

She has presented at a variety of conferences, including the International Society for Technology in Education (ISTE), National Middle School Association, Educational Computing Conference of Ontario, and Educon. She has written articles for ISTE's *Learning and Leading* on how teachers can take control of their professional development to directly impact the classroom. Her latest presentation is "On Being a Risk-Taking Teacher," based on her work with ungrading. Her blog explores the challenges of teaching middle school in a digital world.

ANYTHING IS POSSIBLE

SO WHY DO OUR CLASSROOMS HAVE SO MANY LIMITS?

THE WHOLE POINT OF FORMAL EDUCATION IS TO PREPARE FOR OTHER TIMES AND OTHER PLACES, NOT JUST TO GET BETTER IN THE CLASSROOM. WHAT WE LEARN TODAY IS NOT FOR TODAY BUT FOR THE DAY AFTER TOMORROW. SOMETIMES THE DAY AFTER TOMORROW IS PRETTY MUCH THE SAME AS TODAY, BUT IT VERY OFTEN ISN'T.

—DAVID PERKINS (2012, P. 12)

I now sit on an airplane with my laptop connected to airline-friendly high speed Internet. From a tiny chair thousands of feet in the air, I'm tweeting casually with colleagues in South Carolina, Indonesia, and Philadelphia while watching the latest viral video on YouTube.

Through a chance meeting on a New York City subway, I found an educator who was as passionate about career-focused curriculum as I was. We quickly connected using a Google Doc and sketched out an entire taxonomy of competencies linked to the most popular careers as defined by the Occupational Outlook Handbook.

Recently, Google created glasses that record, search, and compute in response to your verbal cues. Named Google Glass, each pair has more power in a tiny, wearable chip than the computers that put a man on the Moon. I snagged a pair and used them to capture teaching and learning through an educator's eyes.

See? Anything is possible.

Just a few years ago, the things that we currently consider to be normal, everyday activities would have seemed outlandish or odd. Digital networks across the world have enabled the masses to communicate, share, and publish their ideas with unfettered fervor. We live in a world where access to the global community is available via the click of a button. Such uncertainty and unbridled progress can be wonderful. Consider this insightful tweet from David Warlick (see Figure 1.1).

FIGURE 1.1   A TWEET FROM DAVID WARLICK

David Warlick 🐦
@dwarlick

From yesterday's backchannel: "Uncertainty is not bad. 'When anything can happen, then anything is possible.'"

2:37 AM - 19 Feb 2013

SOURCE: Used with permission of David Warlick.

However, our classrooms haven't kept pace with the empowerment that has infiltrated modern reality. In many cases, students attend schools and classes that erect barriers to engagement with meaningful work.

Consider this:

Every day, students go home and hear this question from their parents: What did you learn today?

Often, the answer is "NOTHING."

Perhaps this anecdotal evidence doesn't convince you. Unfortunately, there's more to this story than parents' dinner table reports. According to Organization for Economic Cooperation and Development's 2002 "Education at a Glance Report," one out of every two students worldwide reported that they feel bored at school. In America specifically, 61% of students reported feeling bored at school very often.

In many cases, our desire to protect and manage students has fostered the cultivation of schools that more closely resemble prisons than incubators of innovation.

On a recent walk through a school in Ohio, I noted the following signs posted prominently throughout the building:

- No cell phones!
- No food or drink!
- No iPods or iPads!
- No groups in the hall!
- No talking while the teacher is talking!

At the end of my visit, the only question I had was this: What can you actually *do* in this school?

The limits we have created in schools, albeit well meaning, hold our students back and stifle motivation and mastery.

And while this information might tempt us to blame the institution of school, the kids themselves, or the policy makers, naming an enemy doesn't generate a solution.

But, don't despair. There's a lot that *we* can do to fix this situation *now*. As teachers, we have direct control over the design of our learning setting and the design of our instruction. This is the most powerful weapon we have against boredom and disengagement. Knowing that most teachers I meet are amazing people, I bet you're already making some powerful changes to help your students find connections between their lives and your classroom.

The goal of this book is to provide you with ways to unleash the superpowers of your students. Through specific instructional journeys that fit into the course of your regular day, you can effectively tear down unnecessary limits and show your students that just about anything is possible. I use these instructional journeys (or variations of them) all the time, and it has changed the way that I feel about school, learning, and education.

The student superpowers are as follows:

- Wondering
- Curating
- Connecting

- Digital inking
- Designing
- Gaming

Emphasizing the student superpowers shared in this book isn't difficult, and it doesn't require more preparation than traditional lessons. Using the superpowers just reframes many of our long-held assumptions about what teaching and learning looks like. In short, they require students to do the heavy lifting instead of the teacher.

So join me as we explore ways to have students develop their learning superpowers while realizing that school *is* a place where anything is possible! But first, we must consider why we go to school at all.

WHAT'S THE POINT OF SCHOOL?

Let's start at the beginning by considering a simple question. Why do we go to school?

I actually asked this question to a random group of K–12 students. My favorite responses included:

- "I go to school so my parents don't get in trouble. I actually like my parents."
- "I go to school because I have to."
- "I go to school because I don't have a job yet."
- "I go to school to see my friends."
- "I go to school because I like to play sports after school, and I can't play sports if I don't go to school."
- "I go to school so that I can move out of this town and go to college!"

As these student responses suggest, students aren't seeing the links between school and the real world. Will Richardson, respected blogger and author, recently questioned conventional schooling in his book *Why School?* He said,

> I'm suggesting that this moment requires us to think deeply about why we need school. Or to ask, more specifically, what's the value of school now that opportunities for learning without it are exploding all around us? There is an important, compelling answer to that question. It is most definitely not the same one. (Richardson, 2012)

As the world changes, so does the role of school. Instead of school being a place where we *get stuff,* it must become a place where we *create powerful stuff.* This simple shift will keep school relevant for our students and our society.

To this end, we need to alter our instructional strategies and beliefs about the classroom to better meet the needs of what the Australian Curriculum Studies Association (n.d.) describes as "school leavers," or those who finish school and go forth to make society better.

So, take a moment of pause right now. Why do we have school? Answer this question in the space below:

_____

_____

_____

_____

THE KNOWING-DOING GAP

It's likely that everything you've read up to this point is familiar to you in some way. Perhaps you recognize the superpowers that your students have, and you regularly encourage them. Given the things shared in the news each day and the ways that our students behave, these ideas and concepts are likely familiar to you. However, there is often a considerable gap between what we know and what we actually do in our classrooms.

For example, many years ago I learned that popcorn reading was bad for learning and bad for kids. I had read the research, and I was acutely aware that it did not promote deep thinking for students. However, I continued to use it as a strategy for about 5 months after learning this. Why did I do this? In short, it had become a habit, and the kids *seemed* to like it. However, one day, a student came up to me after class and asked me to reread the entire science selection to him. "Why?" I asked. He calmly said, "When we popcorn read, I get so nervous that I can't remember anything." Well, that instantly broke my bad habit! Sometimes, the literature refers to this phenomenon as the *implementation gap.*

One of the things that can decrease the implementation gap is having a clear plan with short-term wins. Consider this book as your day-to-day plan to narrow the chasm between what you know about students and what you do in your day-to-day practice. Each superpower you foster in your students should be celebrated as a short-term win that creates lasting change for your students!

TEACHERS ARE DESIGNERS

IDEO, a nationally renowned product design company, has recently been using its design process with teachers to help them think flexibly while making constant adjustments for their end users (students!). IDEO's work has affected many of the common products that we use today, and it has also influenced the work of Grant Wiggins and Jay McTighe, authors of *Understanding by Design* (Wiggins & McTighe, 2013). I consider assuming the role of a teacher-designer to be an essential part of the modern teaching profession.

On their website for teachers, IDEO (n.d.) describes the design process for teachers as follows:

> Design Thinking is the confidence that everyone can be part of creating a more desirable future, and a process to take action when faced with a difficult challenge. That kind of optimism is well needed in education.
>
> Classrooms and schools across the world are facing design challenges every single day, from teacher feedback systems to daily schedules. Wherever they fall on the spectrum of scale—the challenges educators are confronted with are real, complex, and varied. And as such, they require new perspectives, new tools, and new approaches. Design Thinking is one of them. (© IDEO LP 2014. All rights reserved.)

Each journey within this text was developed and tested using the design process described by IDEO. This means that each journey in its current state should be considered as a starting point for further refinement and polish. Designers never complete a task; they simply find a point where they're ready to share their ideas with the world. We can improve our classrooms and our instruction by tinkering like a designer.

I'M BUSY! WHERE DOES THIS FIT?

Today, there are more demands on a teacher's time than ever before. In many cases, schools and districts have imposed pacing guides, interim assessments, and rigid, scripted curriculum materials on teachers. If you feel those pressures in your current teaching situation, you are not alone. So, how can the instructional journeys and student superpowers presented in this book be used in your classroom?

As every teaching situation and classroom is unique, it is important to note that there is no "single correct way" to use the ideas and materials presented in this text. In fact, you are encouraged to adapt and tweak each instructional journey to meet your needs. Consider the following principles to guide your implementation:

- **Start small.** You don't have to begin by implementing an instructional journey or student superpower from this book in its entirety. Find a lesson or series of lessons that you'd like to try as a starting point. Experiment with at least one thing that resonates with you. Small successes will encourage you to keep going!

- **Begin by choosing a superpower that complements and satisfies your current requirements.** It's not necessary to teach the superpowers presented in this book in any particular order. Take all the constraints of your current curriculum into account. What units have specific links to the ideas presented in this book? For example, could you teach the Digital Inking Superpower during the time when you normally teach personal narratives as dictated by the pacing guide? Finding these connections can help you satisfy the district requirements while allowing students to truly do the heavy lifting.

- **Use specific content from your pacing guide or curriculum map as a specific focus for one of the superpowers.** Do you have to teach a unit on the regions of your state? Or plants? Or rocks and minerals? Well, then, use these content areas as a lens for one of the superpowers. For example, teach the "questioning superpower" by exploring everything there is to know about plants. Or, teach the "connecting superpower" when you are scheduled to teach the regions of your state. You can accomplish the same goals in many different ways. Consider the superpowers in this book as an engaging way to spice up your requirements!

- **Think about ways to use time flexibly by teaching literacy, science, and social studies at the same time using the student superpowers.** Each instructional journey within this book provides students with several opportunities to demonstrate a complex performance that incorporates many different standards. So, if you only have a very brief allotted period in your day for science or social studies, consider using one of these instructional journeys during *both* your literacy and your science/social studies block. Not only will this give students longer periods of time to grapple with meaningful tasks, but it will also make the day seem more connected and relevant to students.

By thinking flexibly, you'll find many ways to use the materials presented in this book within the constraints of your current situation.

RESEARCH REMINDERS

All of the superpowers in this book have been heavily influenced by leading voices in the field of education, including Ralph Tyler, David Perkins, Robert Marzano, Mike Schmoker, and John Hattie. Each of these authors stresses the need for students to spend more time *actively doing* than *passively listening.* After reading and rereading the works of these authors at different points in my educational career, I've arrived at five fundamental research-based beliefs about teaching and learning that strongly influence each superpower in this book.

1. THE PERSON DOING THE WORK IS DOING THE LEARNING.

If you analyzed each action in your classroom for an entire day, who would be the busiest? Would it be you? Would it be your students? The research tells us that our students should be doing as much of the work as possible. John Hattie, respected researcher and author of the iconic text *Visible Learning,* has dedicated his life to measuring which teacher moves and student moves generate the highest levels of academic achievement. He summarizes his research saying,

> What is most important is that teaching is visible to the student, and that the learning is visible to the teacher. The more the student becomes the teacher and the more the teacher becomes the learner, then the more successful are the outcomes. (Hattie, 2009, p. 25)

Hattie (2009) also reminds us that student self-assessment is the single most powerful strategy to accelerate student achievement. As students learn to use their superpowers, they will learn to self-assess and self-monitor their growing strength and capabilities.

2. FOCUSING ON THE ACQUISITION OF FACTS DOESN'T WORK.

Although many of the tests and assignments that we administer in school simply require students to memorize and regurgitate facts, this strategy doesn't lead to lasting learning. Decades ago, Ralph Tyler warned of this very problem, saying,

> Hence, it is more economical to set up learning situations in which the information is obtained as a part of a total process of problem solving than it is to set up special learning experiences just to memorize information. Furthermore, when information is acquired as a part of problem solving, the use of the information and the reasons for obtaining it are clear. This is less likely to result in rote memorization. (Tyler, 2010, p. 73)

3. TRANSFER IS THE POINT OF EDUCATION, AND TRANSFER IS HARD.

Transfer is defined as one's ability to use skills and information independently in a novel context. It's why we teach: so our students can use what we've taught them long after they leave us. However, the path to transfer has been riddled with failure over the last 100 years. A review of the research reveals that transfer is difficult to achieve, but it's not impossible. A recent meta-analysis report from the National Academies Press called *Education for Life and Work* states: "Research to date suggests that despite our desire for broad forms of transfer, knowledge does not transfer very readily, but it also illuminates instructional conditions that support forms of transfer that are desirable and attainable" (National Research Council, 2012, p. 71).

It is important to note that there are two different types of transfer: specific and general. Specific transfer, sometimes called near transfer, happens when learning is used in two different situations, but commonalities exist. General transfer, on the other hand, happens when the initial learning broadly applies to lots of different situations or contexts. Obviously, general transfer is the ultimate goal, and it is no easy feat!

4. ASKING QUESTIONS IS MORE IMPORTANT THAN FINDING ANSWERS.

In school, we often reward students who generate the correct answers. (Or perhaps, more specifically, the answers that we're looking for.) This certainly doesn't promote divergent or creative thinking. To this end, we need to value problem finding more than problem solving. Consider the wise words of David Perkins (2012):

> Problem finding concerns figuring out what the problems are in the first place. It also involves coming to good formulations of problems, formulations that make them approachable. Often it also involves redefining a problem halfway through trying to solve it, out of the suspicion that one may not be working on quite the right problem. (p. 26)

5. AUTHENTIC LITERACY HAS TO HAPPEN ALL DAY, EVERY DAY.

Fads come and go in education, but authentic literacy never goes out of style. Engaging students in reading and writing for real purposes is almost always a factor that distinguishes successful classrooms from mediocre ones. Citing the need for literacy to touch every subject area, Mike Schmoker wrote a book called *Focus* that explored the unparalleled need for teachers to help students read, write, and discuss. In the text he says, "Literacy is still the unrivalled, but grossly under-implemented, key to learning both content and thinking skills. But authentic literacy is categorically different from the so-called 'reading skills' and pseudo-standards that have wrought such havoc in language arts" (Schmoker, 2011, p. 11).

Authentic literacy happens when students have choice over their texts, they passionately debate the ideas in the text, and they write thoughtfully about it. All of these things should happen regardless of the subject area.

Which research reminder or researcher really resonates with you? Jot your ideas in the space below:

_____

_____

_____

_____

WHAT ABOUT THE STANDARDS?

Regardless of where you teach, you are likely accountable to a set of academic standards. However, the standards tell us *what to teach*, not *how to teach*. Think of the standards as final destination on your GPS. You, as the teacher, can choose any road, route, or path to get to that destination. This is a critical distinction. Educators have the right to use any strategies, methods, or protocols they deem fit to meet the demands of the standards. That's why teaching is so much fun!

Each of the day-to-day instructional journeys in this book is aligned to both the Common Core State Standards for Reading, Writing, and Speaking and Listening and the National Curriculum Standards for Social Studies. Also, there are connections within each journey to several Common Core State Standards of Math Practice.

ALL ABOUT THE
COMMON CORE STATE STANDARDS

The creation of the Common Core State Standards was a state-led effort that included input from teachers, administrators, and experts. The National Governor's Association for Best Practices and the Council of Chief State School Officers coordinated the effort. The standards were designed based upon the strongest components of existing state standards as well as cutting edge research. They are also informed by the practices of other top-performing countries to intentionally reflect the needs of our existing global economy (National Governors Association Center for Best Practices, Council of Chief State School Officers, 2010).

Honestly, this is an incredibly exciting time in education. After years of diluting the standards at the state level in an effort to comply with the regulations of No Child Left Behind (NCLB), the stakes are finally rising again. To use the words of Marzano (2003), "All kids deserve a guaranteed and viable curriculum." The Common Core State Standards seek to provide *just that*.

The authors of the Common Core State Standards have shown a strong movement away from basic acquisition. Instead of focusing on the facts and discrete qualities of literature (Really, how many syllables does a haiku have?), the Common Core State Standards focus on analysis and the derivation of meaning. For example, instead of a focus on identifying different types of figurative language (as is common in most state standard documents), the Common Core State Standards require students to "Interpret words and phrases as they are used in a text, including determining technical, connotative, and figurative meanings, and analyze how specific word choices shape meaning or tone." In many cases, the demands of the Common Core State Standards hearken back to deep comprehension or expression (National Governors Association Center for Best Practices, Council of Chief State School Officers, 2010).

In many ways, this is a huge relief as well as a call to action. Growing students' superpowers will help them meet Common Core benchmarks and expectations.

COMMON CORE STATE STANDARDS FOR READING, WRITING, AND SPEAKING AND LISTENING

Standards that are prioritized throughout an entire instructional journey are labeled as "FOCUS," and standards that are referenced are marked with an "X." Use Figures 1.2, 1.3, and 1.4 as an easy reference for lesson planning.

NATIONAL CURRICULUM STANDARDS FOR SOCIAL STUDIES

Standards that are prioritized throughout an entire instructional journey are labeled as "FOCUS," and standards that are referenced are marked with an "X." Use Figure 1.5 as an easy reference for lesson planning.

COMMON CORE STATE STANDARDS OF MATH PRACTICE

The Common Core State Standards of Math Practice help students engage in problem solving, visualization, and perseverance. Each instructional journey is connected to several Standards of Math Practice. Use Figure 1.6 as an easy reference for lesson planning.

FIGURE 1.2 COMMON CORE STATE STANDARDS FOR READING

	Wondering Journey	Curating Journey	Connecting Journey	Digital Inking Journey	Designing Journey	Gaming Journey
Reading Anchor Standard 1	FOCUS					
Reading Anchor Standard 2				X		
Reading Anchor Standard 3						
Reading Anchor Standard 4						
Reading Anchor Standard 5						
Reading Anchor Standard 6						
Reading Anchor Standard 7	FOCUS					
Reading Anchor Standard 8						
Reading Anchor Standard 9						
Reading Anchor Standard 10		X	X			X

FIGURE 1.3 COMMON CORE STATE STANDARDS FOR WRITING

	Wondering Journey	Curating Journey	Connecting Journey	Digital Inking Journey	Designing Journey	Gaming Journey
Writing Anchor Standard 1						
Writing Anchor Standard 2						FOCUS
Writing Anchor Standard 3						
Writing Anchor Standard 4			FOCUS	FOCUS	X	FOCUS
Writing Anchor Standard 5			X			X
Writing Anchor Standard 6			FOCUS	FOCUS		X
Writing Anchor Standard 7	X	FOCUS				
Writing Anchor Standard 8	X					
Writing Anchor Standard 9						
Writing Anchor Standard 10						

FIGURE 1.4 COMMON CORE STANDARDS FOR SPEAKING AND LISTENING

	Wondering Journey	Curating Journey	Connecting Journey	Digital Inking Journey	Designing Journey	Gaming Journey
Speaking and Listening Anchor Standard 1	X	X	X	X	X	X
Speaking and Listening Anchor Standard 2	X	X	X	X	X	X
Speaking and Listening Anchor Standard 3	X	X	X	X	X	X
Speaking and Listening Anchor Standard 4	X					
Speaking and Listening Anchor Standard 5					X	
Speaking and Listening Anchor Standard 6						

FIGURE 1.5   NATIONAL CURRICULUM STANDARDS FOR SOCIAL STUDIES

	Wondering Journey	Curating Journey	Connecting Journey	Digital Inking Journey	Designing Journey	Gaming Journey
Culture		X	X	X		
Time, Continuity, and Change						
People, Places, and Environments			X			X
Individual Development and Identity		X	X	X		
Individuals, Groups, and Institutions						
Power, Authority, and Governance						X
Production, Distribution, and Consumption					FOCUS	
Science, Technology, and Society	X					
Global Connections	X					
Civic Ideals and Practices	X					

15

FIGURE 1.6 COMMON CORE STATE STANDARDS OF MATH PRACTICE

	Wondering Journey	Curating Journey	Connecting Journey	Digital Inking Journey	Designing Journey	Gaming Journey
SMP 1	X	X	X	X	X	X
SMP 2	X					
SMP 3						
SMP 4					X	
SMP 5		X				
SMP 6						
SMP 7						
SMP 8						

LOOK BACK AND STEP FORWARD

By the end of this introductory chapter, you should feel confident with the following concepts:

- Schools don't always reflect the promise and the problems of real life.
- The student superpowers and instructional journeys in this book can narrow the gap between what we know about learning and your specific classroom experience.
- The design of each student superpower and instructional journey is heavily influenced by educational research and can be implemented within the current constraints teachers face.
- The student superpowers and instructional journeys are aligned to the standards.

• •

A QUESTION TO CONSIDER AS YOU REFLECT

- What do our classrooms need to look like to prepare students for the realities they will face after graduation?

CH.

2

THE STUDENT SUPERPOWERS

As shared in Chapter 1, there are six student superpowers that we need to unleash:

- Wondering
- Curating
- Connecting
- Digital inking
- Designing
- Gaming

THE STUDENT SUPERPOWERS

THE WONDERING STUDENT SUPERPOWER

The Wondering Student Superpower happens when students ask thoughtful questions that may or may not have singular answers. By encouraging kids to wonder, we ask them to think carefully about their environment, their interactions, and their reality.

THE CURATING STUDENT SUPERPOWER

The Curating Student Superpower happens when students synthesize information from various sources to generate understanding and new ideas. Students can seek in many different places, both in person and digital.

THE CONNECTING STUDENT SUPERPOWER

The Connecting Student Superpower happens when students consider their own point of view as well as those of others. Students share their own experiences and learn from the experiences of others.

THE DIGITAL INKING STUDENT SUPERPOWER

The Digital Inking Student Superpower happens when students create digital text and media that can be shared in viral ways. Students spread their messages, thoughts, and ideas with the world!

THE DESIGNING STUDENT SUPERPOWER

The Designing Student Superpower happens when students create and build solutions collaboratively. Using the question stem "What if?" students consider all of the possibilities and navigate existing tensions.

THE GAMING STUDENT SUPERPOWER

The Gaming Student Superpower happens when students motivate and energize people to learn or do work. Designing a learning or practice situation not only requires a high degree of understanding, but it also necessitates critical analysis of texts, people, and situations.

These six student superpowers are ways that we can foster student-driven classrooms. By focusing on each superpower via specific instructional journeys, you can start to see how to implement these superpowers in your classroom.

WHAT IS AN INSTRUCTIONAL JOURNEY? HOW DOES IT PROMOTE STUDENT SUPERPOWERS?

This book is filled with practical, specific instructional journeys that you can use in your classroom to promote each student superpower described above. The instructional journeys seek to answer the question, "How do I do that?"

So, for the sake of clarity, we'll be using the following definition for an instructional journey throughout this text.

An instructional journey is

- A goal-driven sequence of study that requires students to engage in complex performance for an authentic audience and encourages them to develop one of the student superpowers

An instructional journey must include the following:

- Goals that matter to both *kids* and *adults*
- An intentional design that promotes a specific student superpower

- A performance-based assessment that provides direct evidence of progress toward learning goals
- A series of learning activities that help students acquire and make meaning of knowledge and skills
- Intentionally designed opportunities for students to practice the transfer of skills and knowledge *before* the final performance assessment

Instructional journeys can vary in length, but most of the instructional journeys presented in this book will last between *2 and 3 weeks*. You can certainly adjust the length of each journey to meet the needs of your current situation and your learners. You can also combine various parts to emphasize more than one student superpower at once in your classroom.

It's important to note that the format of an instructional journey is very flexible. You may use a different template in your district, and that is perfectly fine. It's about the thinking and design, not filling in specific boxes!

Given the definition and clarifications above, there are many materials we use as teachers that do *not* qualify as instructional journeys. Consider the examples below.

An instructional journey is *not*

- Reading a chapter in a textbook
- Covering content-based topic (the Civil War, the equivalent fractions, etc.)
- Completing a series of standards or skills
- Creating a map or list of everything that you have to cover in a given quarter or school year

While there is certainly some value in materials described above, it is critical to note that these resources were not specifically designed to promote complex student performance. In many cases, the items listed above will actually *prevent* critical thinking and creativity. In many cases, the resources described above result in passive learning experiences for kids.

Let's look at a common example more closely: reading a chapter in a textbook. If a chapter in a textbook serves as the core component of your instruction, you'll likely focus on having students read, tell, and memorize the most important topics or concepts presented in the chapter. With this format, students will acquire facts. However, there's no guarantee that they'll be able to use this information on their own after they graduate. In fact, lots of research shows that most students and adults remember only a few of the facts they learn during their K–12 schooling (Gagne & White, 1978)!

Here's one more example for good measure: completing a series of standards or skills. Many districts and schools break down the Common Core State Standards into hundreds (and even thousands) of skills and behaviors. Then, these skills are carefully portioned into quarters or semesters. Teachers who use these lists as the core component of their instruction certainly ensure that they "cover" all the standards and meet accountability requirements. However, if students don't see how these skills link together via a real-world task or problem, then it's very unlikely that they'll be able to use these skills when presented with an unfamiliar task or standardized assessment (National Research Council, 2012).

THE SUPERPOWERS ARE BIGGER THAN SPECIFIC JOURNEYS

Every superhero's power helps them along thousands of different journeys. It's not related to a single challenge or event. Each of the journeys in this book is a single example. Our hope is that these will be actionable next steps as well as inspirations for future designs.

As you look at each journey in this book, use it as a roadmap that you can generalize to your own teaching and planning. For example, what do you notice about each superpower? How could you tweak or alter your current classroom routines to better emphasize the generalizations you notice?

Identifying the generalizations that belie each example is a great task for a professional learning community or collegial book club. As you work together investigating the general principles of the six student superpowers, you can build a shared understanding of what classrooms should embrace in today's age.

DEBUNKING DEPARTMENTALIZATION

You may or may not have departmentalization in your school. Regardless of the schedule structure that exists where you teach, it's important for students to see learning as a holistic problem-finding *and* problem-solving process. It's less about the schedule and more about how the learning is organized.

Recently, a third-grade learner who goes to a school where each subject is departmentalized shared her experiences. Students switch teachers at three different points throughout the day. As she chatted, she spent most of the time talking about *transitions*. She intricately described how she had "getting started" work (which sounds similar to traditional bell work) and exit tickets at the end of each class. When she talked about math, she mentioned, "I don't mind it that much because it is only 42 minutes." When asked how she used math in science class, she glibly replied, "Well, we get to use our ruler in both subjects. Duh."

The student superpowers and journeys in this book try to help students see connections between ideas, disciplines, and subject areas. Each journey is aligned to standards in reading, writing, speaking, listening, social studies, and science. You are encouraged to use time flexibly as you pursue these standards simultaneously.

If you teach in a self-contained classroom, you can likely reorganize your schedule to accommodate the journeys and superpowers quite easily. However, if you teach in a departmentalized setting, you may need to collaborate with several other teachers to do justice to the student superpowers and journeys in this book. It's a fantastic opportunity to plan collaboratively and ensure that students see direct links between the different subject areas!

As teachers, we can't be expected to know everything. However, we can encourage students to find and explore everything they want to know!

INCLUDED COMPONENTS OF EACH INSTRUCTIONAL JOURNEY

This section will briefly describe all of the components included for each instructional journey that follows.

SUPERPOWER SUMMARY AND OVERVIEW

Each journey begins with a brief summary of the superpower it embodies, providing context to the educator. This section also provides a rationale for the ways that the goals, lessons, and assessments are crafted. This section also specifically references researchers and thought leaders in education as a justification for the overall design.

INSTRUCTIONAL JOURNEY AT A GLANCE

For easy reference, a brief table is provided that summarizes the major components of each instructional journey. Using this chart, you can check on the strength of each superpower for each lesson, links to tech upgrades, standards, and the final assessment.

INSTRUCTIONAL JOURNEY GOALS

The beginning of this chapter noted that an instructional journey is defined by the inclusion of goals that demand complex student performance. This section of the journey states the goals. These goals can (and should!) be shared with students.

STUDENT-FRIENDLY AUTHENTIC LEARNING PROBLEM

Each superpower is taught through a compelling problem or question. You can post this in the classroom to generate interest for the learning activities.

GENERAL PROGRESSION

In three lines, this section explains the conceptual underpinnings of the unit. You can see how each understanding grows and builds throughout the lesson sequence.

CONNECTING THE STANDARDS

This section shows you the standards that are linked to the journey and the student superpower. Focus standards are emphasized, and spiraling complexity in each focus standard is highlighted so that you can see which skills should be "ramped" up for various grade levels. This section should make any lesson planning required by your district easy to complete!

LEARNING ACTIVITIES AND TECH UPGRADES

This section of the journey provides you with specific lesson plans and lesson materials. Each lesson plan is organized according to what the student does and what the teacher does, paying specific attention to ensuring that the student spends considerable time honing his or her superpower! After each lesson, specific tech upgrades are provided as well as troubleshooting tips to try when students don't seem to be "getting it." A curated Pinterest board is also provided in this section so that you can easily keep all your links and printables in one place! Follow all the Student Superpower Pinterest boards at **http://pinterest.com/ssuperpowers/boards.**

FORMATIVE ASSESSMENT AND TRACKING STUDENT PROGRESS TOWARD GOALS

This section provides you with a tracking sheet based on the goals. The student and the teacher can use this tracking sheet collaboratively to ensure that success will be experienced on the final assessment task!

FINAL ASSESSMENT AND RUBRIC

A final assessment task is described in depth, and a rubric is provided to measure student progress toward the journey goals. These assessments are designed to reflect real world situations that students may face in the future.

DIFFERENTIATION: MEETING THE NEEDS OF ALL LEARNERS

In this section, specific suggestions are provided to increase access to learning for diverse students.

WINDOW INTO THE CLASSROOM

Sometimes, seeing a specific example of implementation can help you make sense of an instructional journey and student superpower. This section shares one teacher's story that has been created from dozens of teacher interviews. The goal of this section is to create a clear picture of what you may see, hear, and feel as you experiment.

A FEW FINAL CONSIDERATIONS

Before you prepare to dive into the six superpowers and instructional journeys that follow this chapter, here are a few final considerations:

- **Remember, the intention is to put the students in control of the learning.** Try to turn over as much power to the students as possible in your classroom when you implement each activity. It will be messy at times, and it will certainly be disorganized at times. That's OK. Let the kids persevere! When work happens, there's hustle, bustle, and noise. That's expected. While it can be tempting to take back some control from the students in an effort to make things more comfortable for you, remember that this robs students of educational transfer and rigor.

- **Building a culture for student-driven learning takes time.** As you require students to take more ownership over their learning, you may encounter a little resistance. This is likely because your students are not used to taking intellectual risks akin to those demanded by the student superpowers. Specifically, students may fear failure or "being wrong." Try to encourage students to take chances in their learning. Praise effort instead of achievement. Slowly, the culture in your classroom will change.

- **Audience matters.** Each assessment is designed so that students interact with real people *besides* the teacher. Once the students realize that they're producing work that matters, they will be more motivated to complete the task.

- **The suggested tech upgrades are tools, not goals.** The tech upgrades suggested for each lesson are tools, not goals. Using these upgrades can help you to deliver the instruction in an interactive, engaging way. However, the integrity of the goals will not be compromised if you opt out of the tech upgrades.

- **Beware of the implementation gap. Make a commitment to take a step for kids.** Don't read this book, put it on your shelf, and do nothing. Even if your change is small, change *something*. This is an epic journey, and every step matters. The smallest shifts can create positive outcomes for students. If you need motivation, help, or support, join our virtual community at **www.studentsuperpowers.com.** We'll be there to guide you and help you get started!

LOOK BACK AND STEP FORWARD

By the end of this chapter, you should feel confident with the following concepts:

- Instructional journeys are designed to promote complex performance, and they provide specific examples of each student superpower in action.

- Each journey follows a logical sequence to make planning easy.

- Life isn't departmentalized, so school shouldn't be either.

● ●

A QUESTION TO CONSIDER AS YOU REFLECT

- Which powers do kids need to succeed?

CH.

3

THE WONDERING INSTRUCTIONAL JOURNEY

WHAT DO YOU WONDER?

SUPERPOWER SUMMARY AND OVERVIEW

The Wondering Student Superpower emphasizes asking powerful questions at the right time. This empowers students to explore meaningful, complex problems! In many ways, asking pertinent questions leads to competency. As students increase the strength of this superpower, the quality of their questions will change. Students' questions will probe more deeply, uncover greater mysteries, and explore complex relationships. Be sure to note these changes as formative assessment during the learning journey.

Specifically, this instructional journey encourages students to examine images, text, websites, and videos from the media. (Some will be real, and others will be fake in an effort to incite some passion.) Howard Rheingold, iconic thinker regarding digital literacy, has termed such critical information consumption as "crap detection." This journey culminates with a student-designed game show that showcases amazing questions!

WONDERING JOURNEY AT A GLANCE

WHAT DO YOU WONDER?

Instructional Journey Goals	1. Ask critical questions about a concept, topic, or event. 2. Gather relevant data about a self-posed question. 3. Determine fact from fiction, even when the situation is unclear or multifaceted.
General Progression	→ The world is *not* transparent. 　→ Asking the right questions can lead us to competency. 　　→ It's up to us to find the right questions!
Connecting the Standards	Common Core State Standards for Reading, Writing, and Speaking and Listening • RI.1—FOCUS STANDARD • RI.7—FOCUS STANDARD • W.7 • W.8 • SL.1 • SL.2 • SL.3 • SL.4 National Curriculum Standards for Social Studies • Science, Technology, and Society • Global Connections • Civic Ideas and Practices Common Core State Standards of Math Practice • SMP 1 • SMP 2
Learning Activities	Lesson 1: What Is Real; What Is Fake? Lesson 2: How Do We Use Questions to Find Answers We Need? Lesson 3: Is This Question Any Good? Lesson 4: Asking My Own Questions and Testing Out My Ideas
Tech Upgrades	• Padlet—www.padlet.com • Bounce—www.bounceapp.com • Socrative—www.socrative.com • Haiku Deck—www.haikudeck.com
Final Assessment	Game Show Redesign

STUDENT-FRIENDLY AUTHENTIC LEARNING PROBLEM

What do you wonder? Sometimes, really good questions help us to find really good answers. However, the *best* questions usually lead us to . . . *more questions!* Over the next few weeks, your job will be to find the *best* questions and build the student superpower of *wondering.* Your questions will be about many different topics that interest you. So, what do you wonder?

GENERAL PROGRESSION

→ The world is *not* transparent.

 → Asking the right questions can lead us to competency.

 → It's up to us to find the right questions!

CONNECTING THE STANDARDS

As this instructional journey and superpower are closely linked to critical literacy, the two focus standards come from the ELA Common Core. Areas that show increasing complexity are underlined for your reference (see the following table).

CONNECTIONS TO OTHER STANDARDS

COMMON CORE STATE STANDARDS FOR READING, WRITING, AND SPEAKING AND LISTENING

- **W.7**—Conduct short as well as more sustained research projects based on focused questions, demonstrating understanding of the subject under investigation.

- **W.8**—Gather relevant information from multiple print and digital sources, assess the credibility and accuracy of each source, and integrate information while avoiding plagiarism.

OVERALL STANDARD	GRADE 3	GRADE 4	GRADE 5
RI.1: Read closely to determine what the text says explicitly and to make logical inferences from it; cite specific textual evidence when writing or speaking to support conclusions drawn from the text.	**RI.1.3:** Ask and answer questions to demonstrate understanding of a text, referring explicitly to the text as the basis for the answers.	**RI.1.4:** Refer to details and examples in a text when explaining what the text says explicitly and when drawing inferences from the text.	**RI.1.5:** Quote accurately from a text when explaining what the text says explicitly and when drawing inferences from the text.
RI.7: Integrate and evaluate content presented in diverse media and formats, including visually and quantitatively, as well as in words.	**RI.7.3:** Use information gained from illustrations (e.g., maps photographs) and the words in a text to demonstrate understanding of the text.	**RI.7.4:** Interpret information presented visually, orally, or quantitatively (e.g., charts graphs, diagrams, timelines, animations, or interactive Web elements) and explain how the information contributes to an understanding of the text in which it appears.	**RI.7.5:** Draw on information from multiple print or digital sources, demonstrating the ability to locate an answer to a question quickly or to solve a problem efficiently.

- **SL.1**—Prepare for and participate effectively in a range of conversations and collaborations with diverse partners, building on others' ideas and expressing their own clearly and persuasively.

- **SL.2**—Integrate and evaluate information presented in diverse media and formats, including visually, quantitatively, and orally.

- **SL.3**—Evaluate a speaker's point of view, reasoning, and use of evidence and rhetoric.

- **SL.4**—Present information, findings, and supporting evidence such that listeners can follow the line of reasoning and the organization, development, and style are appropriate to task, purpose, and audience.

- Science, Technology, and Society
- Global Connections
- Civic Ideas and Practices

COMMON CORE STATE STANDARDS OF MATH PRACTICE

- **SMP 1**—Make sense of problems and persevere in solving them.
- **SMP 2**—Reason abstractly and quantitatively.

LEARNING ACTIVITIES AND TECH UPGRADES

There are four lessons associated with this journey. In this book, lessons are defined as related series of student-driven explorations, not merely what will fit in a single class period. Actually, it is likely that each of these lessons will take several class periods to complete. After students explore all four lessons, provide them with the transfer task that follows to obtain summative data relative to the journey goals. All lesson resources (labeled for easy use) can be found on this Pinterest board:

http://pinterest.com/ssuperpowers/wondering-journey

(You can follow all Student Superpower Pinterest boards at **http://pinterest.com/ssuperpowers/boards**.)

LESSON 1: WHAT IS REAL; WHAT IS FAKE?

For this lesson, students look at several different examples of believable and *unbelievable* media. As a class, students brainstorm questions about what they've seen. These questions begin an emphasis on curiosity that continues throughout the journey.

GENERAL PROCEDURES

1. Arrange students in pairs and remind them to take turns during various discussion points in the lesson.

2. Show the Gmail Motion video available on the Pinterest board for this journey. *Note: This is an April Fool's Joke created by Google.*

3. Students discuss the following questions with their partner followed by a whole-group debrief:

   - What is happening in this video?
   - What is real?
   - What is fake?

4. Show the Waterslide Jump video available on the Pinterest board. *Note: This is a known hoax. It is not real. It was edited by the videographer.*

5. Students discuss the following questions with their partner followed by a whole-group debrief:

   - What is happening in this video?
   - What is real?
   - What is fake?

6. Pass out sticky notes and stickers to students. Prompt students to work in pairs to fill up as many sticky notes as possible with questions that they have about how they determine what is real and what is fake. Depending on the profile of the class, you may wish to model this for students using the examples below:

   - Who made that video?
   - Why would someone want to trick us on the Internet?
   - Does someone check what goes onto the Internet?
   - How do we find out the truth about what we see on the Internet?

7. Students generate questions on pink sticky notes with their partner and place them in a central location in the room. (Putting the sticky notes on a rug that students can gather around works well.) Students are encouraged to keep thinking and brainstorming beyond their first ideas. Often the best ideas come after several minutes of deep thinking!

8. Direct students to gather in a circle around all the sticky notes. Students use stickers to vote for their favorite questions. *Note: This provides the teacher with important formative data about the interests of the class.*

9. Record the "broad labels" for each group of questions on a piece of chart paper or a Smartboard. Examples of labels could include "author," "where you found it," etc. See Figure 3.1 for an example.

FIGURE 3.1

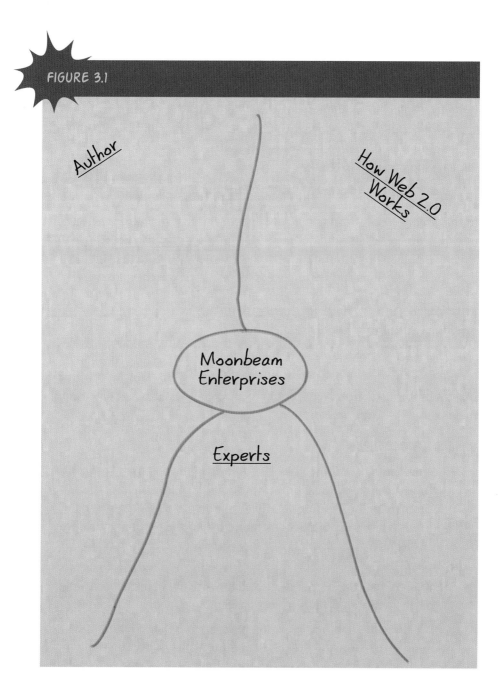

10. Students work as a class to group and label all the sticky notes based on similarities and differences. These "broad labels" help students to build cognitive schema about analyzing media with a critical lens.

11. Tell students that they'll be exploring these "broad labels" as the unit proceeds.

12. Students write an exit ticket that answers the following question:

    At this point, what piques your curiosity? What do you really want to know?

Try using Padlet.com (formerly Wallwisher) instead of sticky notes with students. Padlet allows students to post virtual sticky notes on a virtual board. They can also rearrange the sticky notes to group and label them. Padlet can be used anonymously and without a log in, so it functions in the same way as paper sticky notes!

ARE THEY GETTING IT? POTENTIAL MISCONCEPTIONS AND SNAGS

In this lesson, some students may not understand that people on the Internet intend to deceive us or lie about the truth. Students may also not realize that anyone is able to post information on the Internet. Be on the lookout for these misconceptions and try to discuss them as a class if they arise.

LESSON 2: HOW DO WE USE QUESTIONS TO FIND ANSWERS WE NEED?

Now that the class has some ideas about what to consider when judging if something is real or fake, they will begin a personal investigation with a partner in the class. However, the quality of their questions will determine the quality of the information that they receive!

GENERAL PROCEDURES

1. Show the chart of "broad labels" from the previous day's lesson. One student leads a summary of the previous day's learning. He or she summarizes the learning and then calls on other students to add details. The student leader determines when the summary is sufficient.

2. Distribute paper to students and guide them to create a graphic organizer to be used throughout the lesson. Tell students to create different regions on the paper, and to write the name of each "broad label" at the top of each region. See a sample in Figure 3.2.

3. Tell students that they are going to choose from a series of topics. Some will be real and others will be fake. The teacher shares the following topics with students. These topics can be accessed via the Pinterest board for this instructional journey:

   - Pacific Northwest Tree Octopus (fake)
   - Moonbeam Enterprises (fake)
   - The Federal Vampire and Zombie Agency (fake)
   - California's Velcro Crop (fake)
   - Arabian Oryx (real)
   - Big Fish (real)

4. Students choose a topic based on their interest and record it on their paper.

FIGURE 3.2

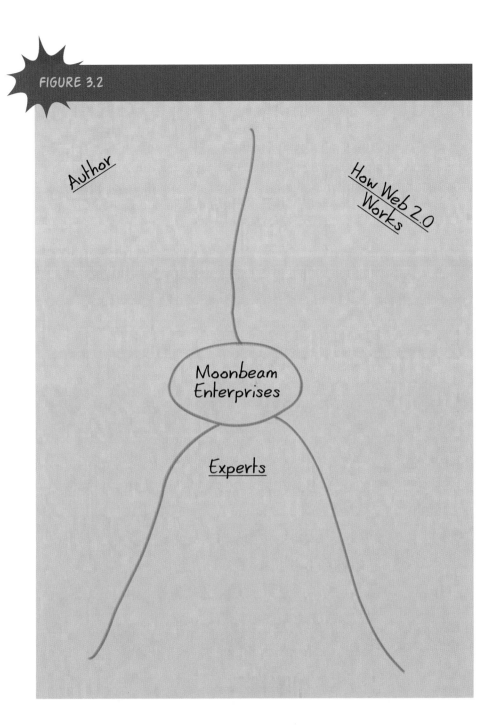

Author

How Web 2.0 Works

Moonbeam Enterprises

Experts

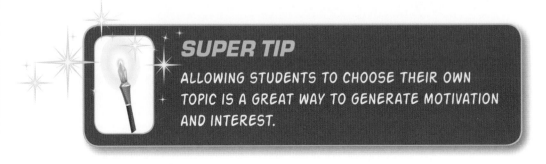

SUPER TIP

ALLOWING STUDENTS TO CHOOSE THEIR OWN TOPIC IS A GREAT WAY TO GENERATE MOTIVATION AND INTEREST.

5. Set up stations around the room for students to explore the websites. If there is no access to computers, you may wish to print out the pages of the websites for students to examine. Provide students with the material they selected based on their interest.

6. Students generate as many questions as possible under each "broad label" while exploring the website they selected. Students write their questions under the appropriate region on their paper. This helps them to consider if they've generated questions about all the important areas. See a sample in Figure 3.3.

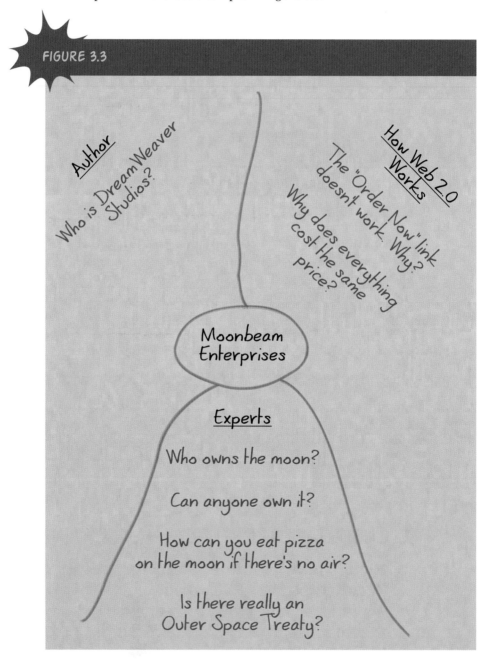

FIGURE 3.3

Author
Who is DreamWeaver Studios?

How Web 2.0 Works
The "Order Now" link doesn't work. Why?
Why does everything cost the same price?

Moonbeam Enterprises

Experts
Who owns the moon?
Can anyone own it?
How can you eat pizza on the moon if there's no air?
Is there really an Outer Space Treaty?

7. Students *swap* their questions with a peer who explored something different. Students have to try to find answers to their peer's questions by exploring the site themselves and doing other research. Students can use the strategies shared by the teacher as well as any other strategies they want to try. Students are encouraged to interact with their peers as they figure out answers to their questions.

8. Introduce three tools that students can use to help them answer their peers' questions:

   - http://www.easywhois.com—This will tell students who owns a site.

   - http://www.alexa.com—This will tell students how many people visit the site.

   - Put "link: the website address" into Google to find out what other sites have linked to the site.

9. Once students have found answers for their peer, they swap papers again. Students carefully examine the information that they have received and try to make a final determination about the site. They can choose from the following options:

   - I think my site is real because . . .

   - I think my site is fake because . . .

   - I'm not sure if my site is real or fake because I didn't ask the right questions. I should have asked . . .

   - I'm not sure if my site is real or fake because I don't understand the answers my partner gave me . . .

10. Students share their judgments with the class. The teacher should not "tell" students which sites are fake and which are real. It is critical to communicate that student work will move the class forward. The teacher can ask probing questions if misconceptions or errors are revealed, but the teacher should *not* position himself or herself as the owner of knowledge. This activity provides excellent formative information to the teacher about students' abilities to ask questions, find information, and make judgments based on that information.

11. Students self-evaluate their performance on the lesson using the three-finger strategy for three tasks: (1) asking good questions; (2) finding good answers; and (3) finding the truth.

    - Students hold up three fingers if they felt they did a *great* job.

    - Students hold up two fingers if they felt they did an OK job.

    - Students hold up one finger if they are really confused and need more help on this task.

Try using Bounce (www.bounceapp.com) as a way for students to generate their questions. This tool allows students to put digital notes on top of any website quickly and easily. Instead of having students write their questions on paper, they can directly annotate a website with this app. They simply paste the URL into Bounce and then they can type their questions directly onto a webpage!

ARE THEY GETTING IT? POTENTIAL MISCONCEPTIONS AND SNAGS

As students generate questions about their topic, they may focus on the content of the site too much. (For example, How many tentacles does a Pacific Northwest tree octopus have?) If this happens, keep reminding students of their goal: to determine if the site is real or fake.

LESSON 3: IS THIS QUESTION ANY GOOD?

At this point in the unit, students are beginning to see the importance of asking the right questions. In this lesson, students will have more freedom to explore all types of questions on many different topics. They'll also develop common criteria that the *best* questions share. Wonderopolis.org will be used to help students uncover wonderings on many different topics. Wonderopolis is an engaging website geared for learners at Grades 3, 4, and 5. It is organized around questions and answers. A link to this site can be found on the Pinterest board for this unit.

GENERAL PROCEDURES

1. The teacher asks students the following question:

    *   What kinds of questions were most helpful in yesterday's lesson? Why?

2. A student leader passes a ball to other students as they share responses to the question. When the student leader feels the question has been answered sufficiently, he or she passes the ball back to the teacher.

SUPER TIP

ALLOWING STUDENTS TO LEAD DISCUSSION PROMOTES EMPOWERMENT.

3. The teacher reminds students that they are trying to become really good question finders (as compared to answer finders). The

teacher introduces Wonderopolis, a site that features question-based investigations.

4. Students explore Wonderopolis in a small group or with a partner. Students select their favorite questions based on personal interest and everything they've learned so far. Students verbally justify their choices to their group members before a particular question or wonder is added to the group's list of "good questions."

5. Each group shares the questions they selected. The entire class selects one question from each group to be added to a class list.

6. The teacher asks students:

   • What do these questions have in common?

7. Students consider what these "good questions" have in common. Students develop a list of criteria about what constitutes a good question. *Note: It will be very tempting for the teacher to begin to prompt students for the criteria. Try to allow students to lead this section of the lesson as much as possible.*

8. Students complete an exit ticket:

   • What makes a good question?

TECH UPGRADE FOR THIS LESSON

Instead of having students record their questions on paper, they can input them into Socrative.com. Socrative is a free Web app that functions as a student response system. This app can be accessed using smartphones, computers, iPads, or iPod Touches. The teacher can create a virtual room. Students can log into this room and share their questions. There is also a rating feature in Socrative where students can vote for their favorite response (or in this case, question).

ARE THEY GETTING IT? POTENTIAL MISCONCEPTIONS AND SNAGS

As we've been focused on real vs. fake for the previous lessons, students may be overly concerned that the content on this site is fake. Certainly encourage students to be careful consumers of the information on the site, and you may even want to use several of the strategies used in the last lesson, such as www.easywhois.com, to verify the authenticity of the site before students begin to evaluate the questions contained on it. However, remember that the thread of this unit shifts from the *need* for good questions to the *qualities* that all good questions share. Try to make that apparent for students, and show them that their detective skills in other lessons helped them to develop better questioning skills.

LESSON 4: ASKING MY OWN QUESTIONS AND TESTING OUT MY IDEAS

In this lesson, students will craft questions that interest them. This is a necessary competency within a student-driven classroom. As this lesson is the final one within this instructional journey, its goal is to provide students with a final opportunity to explore the concept of questioning before the transfer task.

GENERAL PROCEDURES

1. The teacher shares the best questions from yesterday's lesson. Then he or she asks students to identify what made the questions similar.

2. Next, one student begins to recap the previous day's work while holding a ball of yarn. As the student passes the conversation to another student, he or she also passes the ball of yarn. As the ball of yarn unravels, students can visually track the conversation's pathway. (Don't have yarn? This activity also works great with toilet paper!)

3. The teacher reminds students that they are on a quest to find the right *questions* to investigate a topic of their choosing. (You may scaffold topic selection with a list based on your students' needs, classroom curricula, or outside interests.) Teachers may wish to model this for students.

4. Students take 20 minutes of uninterrupted time to begin to brainstorm their questions. It may be best to provide this time either in the library or a place where the access to resources is abundant. Students can generate questions about any topic that interests them, including topics that have been explored in previous lessons.

SUPER TIP

ALWAYS PROVIDE QUIET OR STILL TIME FOR STUDENTS TO THINK AND REFLECT.

5. Students share their questions with a peer. Peers should tell each other which questions they found most interesting.

6. Students rank their questions in order of importance.

7. As an exit ticket, students jot down their top three questions on a sticky note.

TECH UPGRADE FOR THIS LESSON

Haiku Deck is a free iPad app that allows students to make simple, beautiful slide decks. As the app strives to emphasize thinking through visual images, it is the perfect way for students to record their questions and add relevant images. Instead of having students record their questions on paper, have them create a haiku deck for their questions. These are easily sharable online and via social media.

ARE THEY GETTING IT? POTENTIAL MISCONCEPTIONS AND SNAGS

In most cases, the biggest snag with this lesson relates to selecting a topic. Most students will know what they want to question right away, but others may get stuck. A few students may say things like, "I don't know what I want to explore" or "I don't have questions about anything." This often happens, especially in the early stages of a student-run classroom. However, don't get frustrated or give up. More importantly, *do not* give students a topic; rather, provide a range of topics if needed. Help them find something that really interests them. It's likely that their frustration is coming from the fact that they've never been given "free reign" before, and they don't believe that they can question something they truly love or enjoy. Help them through this; it will have big payoffs in the future!

FORMATIVE ASSESSMENT AND TRACKING STUDENT PROGRESS TOWARD GOALS

At the end of each lesson, students should self-assess their progress using the arrow continuum related to each journey goal using a yellow crayon. (See the following Formative Tracking Sheet for the arrow continuum.) You may also wish to have students provide notes or evidence justifying their rating. After students self-evaluate, you should assess their progress using a blue crayon. In every case where your rating agrees with the student's rating, it will create a "green light." This helps students to norm their ability to track their own progress. After using this strategy for some time, you'll likely find that most students are more stringent on their performance than you are!

Not only does this twofold method give you helpful information for future lessons, but it is also a strategy that significantly accelerates student achievement (Hattie, 2009). Go to the Pinterest page for this instructional journey to download the tracking sheet.

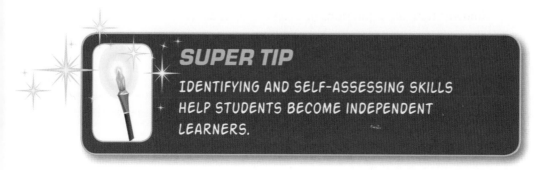

SUPER TIP

IDENTIFYING AND SELF-ASSESSING SKILLS HELP STUDENTS BECOME INDEPENDENT LEARNERS.

FORMATIVE TRACKING SHEET: WHAT DO YOU WONDER?

Formative Tracking Sheet: What Do You Wonder?

What do you wonder? Sometimes, really good questions help us to find really good answers. However, the BEST questions usually lead us to . . . MORE QUESTIONS! Over the next few weeks, your job will be to find the BEST questions. These questions will be about many different things that interest you. So, what do you wonder?

Unit Goals:

GOAL 1:
Ask pointed questions about a concept, topic, or event.

GOAL 2:
Gather relevant data about a self-posed question.

GOAL 3:
Determine fact from fiction, even when the situation is unclear.

Learning Target for Goal 1: I can ask good questions.

Lesson 1:
Exit Ticket: At this point, what piques your curiosity? What do you really want to know?

Lesson 2:
Exit Ticket: Did your questions provide you with enough information to figure out if your site was real or fake?

Lesson 3:
Exit Ticket: What makes a good question?

Lesson 4:
Exit Ticket: Your Top Three Questions

Rate your own mastery of this learning target after each lesson. Remember that your rating can change over time:

New to Me ⟵————————————————————⟶ I Got This!

Learning Target for Goal 2: I can find information about a question I have.

Lesson 2:
Lesson Task: Could you find answers to your peer's question?

Lesson 3:
Lesson Task: Could you find answers to interesting questions on Wonderopolis?

Rate your own mastery of this learning target. Remember that your rating can change over time:

New to Me ⟵————————————————————⟶ I Got This!

Learning Target for Goal 3: I can figure out when something is real or fake.

Lesson 1:
Lesson Task: Could you figure out if each video was real or fake?

Lesson 2:
Lesson Task: Could you figure out if the website you selected was real or fake?

Rate your own mastery of this learning target. Remember that your rating can change over time:

New to Me ⟵————————————————————⟶ I Got This!

SOURCE: This tool was inspired by a tool shared by Bill Ferriter in a blog post:
http://blog.williamferriter.com/2013/02/16/my-middle-schoolers-actually-love-our-unit-overview-sheets

UNLEASHING STUDENT SUPERPOWERS

FINAL ASSESSMENT: HAVE YOUR GOALS BEEN ACHIEVED?

GAME SHOW REDESIGN

For the final assessment of this unit, all three instructional journey goals are seamlessly integrated into one authentic performance. Essentially, students will create and play a game show in the classroom.

STUDENT-FRIENDLY PROMPT

It's game time! Now that you are a master of crafting and answering the *best* questions, you have all the skills you need to design and play a new game show. Alec Trebek, the host of *Jeopardy!,* has asked you to help him try out a new show. He's bored with the constant question-answer routine. So, you need to mix it up. First, you will generate some fantastic questions and find as much information as you can about each question. From there, we'll play the game. Here's what it will look like:

- There will be five to seven contestants on stage at one time with questions and answers/information/research in response to those questions.

- The first contestant will take a turn sharing information that he or she discovered in his or her research. This information may be *true* or *false.*

  - The audience will generate as many questions as possible about the topic. The audience can submit their questions via Socrative or using index cards.

  - If an audience question matches a question that the contestant had generated, both players get 100 points.

  - Then all players get 5 minutes to find answers to their questions and determine if the piece of information is true or false. (It usually works best for students to do this step in teams of three to four.)

  - Players share their judgment about the fact and back it up with evidence that they found.

  - The contestant either affirms or denies the truth of the shared information. 100 points are awarded to players who arrive at a correct judgment. 100 points are awarded to the contestant if the player makes an incorrect judgment.

- Play continues with each contestant taking a turn. (You may need to play several "games" so that everyone gets an opportunity to be a contestant.)

- Points are tallied at the end of the game.

RUBRIC INDICATOR	SUPERHERO	SIDEKICK	APPRENTICE
Finding Questions	You are able to create open-ended questions that could have many answers.	You are able to create some open-ended questions and some questions that have only a single answer.	You can think of questions.
Finding Evidence	You are able to compare information from several sources to help you learn about your questions.	You are able to find information from several sources to help you learn about your questions.	You are able to find information to help you learn about your questions.
Making a Judgment	You are able to use several sources of information to make accurate judgments about the truth of a piece of information.	You are able to use information from a single source to make accurate judgments about the truth of a piece of information.	Sometimes you find it challenging to make accurate judgments about the truth of a piece of information.

DIFFERENTIATION: MEETING THE NEEDS OF ALL LEARNERS

All classrooms have a wide variety of learners. It's necessary to make specific changes to our instruction to ensure that all students can access the instructional journey goals. Here are a few strategies for this instructional journey to remove barriers to learning that may exist for some students.

Provide students with question stems. If students are struggling with the language skills required to frame a good question, you may want to provide them with question stems. These starters can help students better express their ideas in spite of language needs. Question stems could include:

- What if . . .
- To what extent . . .
- How can . . .

Give students examples and nonexamples of good questions. Some students may not be able to use the criteria created by the class to analyze questions. If this happens, you may want to provide students with specific examples and nonexamples. An explicit concept-attainment lesson can go a long way in supporting students who struggle with this skill.

Allow students to peer coach each other. Students who need extra support during different activities can benefit from a peer coaching system. The system can be based on the information recorded on the formative assessment tracking sheet. If students feel that they've "got it" regarding an instructional journey goal, then they can have the opportunity to peer coach someone who "needs more help." This can be an informal or formal process, depending on the needs of your students and your classroom profile.

WINDOW INTO THE CLASSROOM

Jennie is a third-grade teacher in an urban district. She has 19 diverse learners in her class, and each student is reading at a different level. Although Jennie's students are comfortable answering simple questions, they are often intimidated when she asks them open-ended questions. Because of this, Jennie wanted to help her students hone their Wondering Superpower.

Jennie began with Lesson 1. Since Jennie's students work in pairs often, they were able to take turns talking and sharing their ideas. However, some students were certain that the videos were real. Jennie struggled to stay quiet and wait for students to correct other students' misconceptions. In every case except for one, the class was able to correct each other and get the discussion on track. After that lesson, many of the students were very excited to go home and strengthen their superpower by quizzing their parents to find the truth behind each clip.

As Jennie prepared to teach Lesson 2, she had to be very strategic about how she grouped students. Since some students were reading significantly below grade level, she wanted to pair these students with peers who would be able to read the websites. She also planned this lesson for a day when she had access to a guided reading aide so that additional adult support would be available. Students were really excited to ask questions about the sites, and they were also highly motivated to find the truth by answering the questions of a peer. However, some of the students struggled to use the copy/paste function as they tried to use EasyWhoIs and Alexis. Jennie made a note to teach these skills before beginning the lesson in the future. As a class, the students were very successful in identifying the difference between fact and fiction with the lesson.

By the time Jennie got to Lesson 3, she started to notice a change in her students. They were asking more and more questions at all points of the day. The Wondering Superpower was growing in her classroom. During reading and writing, students were posing all sorts of questions. Jennie kept encouraging this, and she started to note their mounting questions on a piece of chart paper in the room. During Lesson 3, the students were ready to collect good questions from Wonderopolis. Much of the text was a little bit below grade level, so all students were able to access it quite easily. However, Jennie was surprised that students were highly critical of the questions on the site. Many even offered suggestions and revisions for the questions on the site, making them more complex. She was thrilled! By the end of Lesson 3, students had uncovered the following criteria for a good question:

1. It doesn't have a single answer.
2. It's about something interesting.
3. It makes you think of other questions.

During Lesson 4, students began brainstorming their own questions using the criteria they had developed in Lesson 3. However, a few students expressed that they didn't know what to ask about. Once Jennie made them realize that they really could ask about *anything* (even Xbox!), they quickly got to work.

Students researched these questions and generated more questions in preparation for their game show. The students were so excited about the game show that Jennie decided to invite their parents to attend. A few parents came to the event, and one even brought snacks for the class as a surprise! The students worked really hard and had a lot of fun asking and researching good questions. All the students in the class were rated as "practitioner" or "master" on the rubric for the final performance task except for two. Those two students worked together to keep practicing the skills during guided reading time.

Jennie learned a lot from the instructional journey, mostly that she needed to take a step back. Jennie's students really enjoyed using the Wondering Superpower. She even had a parent tell her that one student wanted to play the game show during her birthday party!

● ●

A QUESTION TO CONSIDER AS YOU REFLECT

-   What practices do you currently use that emphasize questions with a single right answer? Can you reduce the number of questions with a single right answer asked by you and your students?

4

THE CURATING INSTRUCTIONAL JOURNEY

SOLVING A PUZZLE

SUPERPOWER SUMMARY AND OVERVIEW

The Curating Student Superpower emphasizes making meaning of the world, just like solving a puzzle. "Sources of information are vast and disparate, and individuals crave coherence and integration" (Gardner, 2008, p. 46). It is no longer the job of a librarian to make decisions about information. Each student must know how to identify important sources. Students must be able to categorize what they find clearly, creating their own "personal library" from the mass of information available online.

Rather than being overwhelmed by the masses of information surrounding them, students need to be able to take control of what is available to them. Once they take control, students must categorize these new resources. Young children often do this naturally. "Celebrate, don't censor or curtail the connections that are effortlessly effected by the young mind" (Gardner, 2008, p. 68). This ability is critical in developing a "synthesizing mind for the future," which is at the heart of being a curator.

CURATING JOURNEY AT A GLANCE

SOLVING A PUZZLE

Instructional Journey Goals	1. Recognize important information. 2. Categorize. 3. Synthesize many different sources.

General Progression	→ I am surrounded by information in all sorts of forms.
	    → I can take control over information, organizing it in new and important ways.
	        → I can make connections between people and ideas.

Connecting the Standards	Common Core State Standards for Reading, Writing, and Speaking and Listening
	
	    • W.7—FOCUS STANDARD
	    • R.10
	    • SL.1
	    • SL.2
	    • SL.3
	
	National Curriculum Standards for Social Studies
	    • Culture
	    • Individual Development and Identity
	
	Common Core State Standards of Math Practice
	    • SMP 1
	    • SMP 5

Learning Activities	Lesson 1: What Can I Find? Lesson 2: So Where Does It Go? Lesson 3: Creating New From Old
Tech Upgrades	• Mind mup—http://www.mindmup.com/#m:new • Google Docs—http://docs.google.com • U Roulette — http://www.uroulette.com
Final Assessment	Creating School Clubs

After categorizing, students must share their ideas and their collections with others, becoming budding experts and helping others. Marc Prensky notes in his book, *Teaching Digital Natives* (2010), that today's students are actually researchers and curators. The authors of the Common Core State Standards recognize this as well, emphasizing the need for authentic research. When students become empowered by the curation process, it allows them to research, manage, and share their understanding with the world.

INSTRUCTIONAL JOURNEY GOALS

1. Recognize important information.
2. Categorize.
3. Synthesize many different sources.

STUDENT-FRIENDLY AUTHENTIC LEARNING PROBLEM

Being a curator is like solving a puzzle. It requires lots of investigation and building new solutions from the pieces that you find. With the wealth of information available today, you can build a library that works just for you. You can use it to connect with other people around the world who have similar interests to you or who know things that you don't know and want to learn.

GENERAL PROGRESSION

→ I am surrounded by information in all sorts of forms.

  → I can take control over information, organizing it in new and important ways.

    → I can make connections between people and ideas.

CONNECTING THE STANDARDS

As this instructional journey and superpower are closely linked to critical literacy, the focus standard comes from the ELA Common Core. Areas that show increasing complexity are underlined for your reference (see the following table).

CONNECTIONS TO OTHER STANDARDS

COMMON CORE STATE STANDARDS FOR
READING, WRITING, AND SPEAKING AND LISTENING

- **R.10**—Read and comprehend literary and informational texts independently and proficiently.

CONNECTING THE STANDARDS

OVERALL STANDARD	GRADE 3	GRADE 4	GRADE 5
W.7: Conduct short as well as more sustained research projects based on focused questions, demonstrating understanding of the subject under investigation.	**W.7.3:** Conduct short research projects that build knowledge about a topic.	**W.7.4:** Conduct short research projects that build knowledge through investigation of <u>different aspects</u> of a topic.	**W.7.5:** Conduct short research projects that use <u>several sources</u> to build knowledge through investigation of different aspects of a topic.

- **SL.1**—Prepare for and participate effectively in a range of conversations and collaborations with diverse partners, building on others' ideas and expressing their own clearly and persuasively.

- **SL.2**—Integrate and evaluate information presented in diverse media and formats, including visually, quantitatively, and orally.

- **SL.3**—Evaluate a speaker's point of view, reasoning, and use of evidence and rhetoric.

NATIONAL CURRICULUM STANDARDS FOR SOCIAL STUDIES

- Culture

- Individual Development and Identity

COMMON CORE STATE STANDARDS OF MATH PRACTICE

- **SMP 1**—Make sense of problems and persevere in solving them.

- **SMP 5**—Use appropriate tools strategically.

LEARNING ACTIVITIES AND TECH UPGRADES

There are three lessons associated with this journey. In this book, lessons are defined as related series of student-driven explorations, not merely what will fit in a single class period. Actually, it is likely that each of these lessons will take several class periods to complete. After students explore all three lessons, provide them with the transfer task that follows to obtain summative data relative to the journey goals. All lesson resources (labeled for easy use) can be found on this Pinterest board:

http://pinterest.com/ssuperpowers/curating-journey

(You can follow all Student Superpower Pinterest boards at **http://pinterest.com/ssuperpowers/boards**.)

LESSON 1: WHAT CAN I FIND?

This lesson is a series of investigations, where students are looking for different items. The goal is to recognize the importance of careful observation and listening.

They will be looking at images, listening to sounds, and skimming pages to find specific aspects in each. This is the first step in developing the Curating Superpower.

GENERAL PROCEDURES

1. Introduce the Curating Superpower and give an overview of the steps in the curation process:

   - Identify
   - Categorize
   - Blend
   - Share

2. Arrange a series of stations and explain the tasks at each one to the class:

   - **Words on a Page**. Make copies of a page from a classroom textbook. At the top of the page, write four to five significant words from the page. Have colored markers at the station. Students circle the words when they find them.

   - ***Where's Waldo?*** Borrow three to four of the *Where's Waldo* books from the library. Arrange them at the station. Students try and find Waldo on each page.

   - **Listening for Sounds.** Provide headphones for three to four students. Students play a recording that is familiar to the students or connected to the curriculum. They listen for specific words or instruments. Have them raise a finger when they hear it. For example, play a portion of Tchaikovsky's *1812 Overture* and raise a finger when there are drums or cymbals.

   - **Hidden pictures from www.allkidsnetwork.com/hidden-pictures.** Link also on Pinterest board. Students look for the items at the bottom and circle them when they find them.

3. Hold a whole-group class discussion about the best strategies for identifying *exactly* what you're looking for. Work as a group to create a shared definition of the first phase in the curation process: identifying.

SUPER TIP

OFFERING TASKS THAT USE A VARIETY OF THE
SENSES SUPPORTS LEARNERS' DIVERSE NEEDS.

TECH UPGRADE FOR THIS LESSON

Create visual notes from the whole-group debrief using Mindmup.com to
make a mind map.

ARE THEY GETTING IT? POTENTIAL MISCONCEPTIONS AND SNAGS

Pay close attention to the stations that each student chooses first. It can be
an indication of the senses with which they are the most comfortable.

LESSON 2: SO WHERE DOES IT GO?

This lesson provides the students with opportunities to build categories.
They learn why categories are important and how to arrange information
that they find in the places where it makes the most sense to them
individually.

GENERAL PROCEDURES

1. For this activity, students will be building categories with decks
    of cards. Get eight decks of playing cards. Divide the class into
    eight groups. Hand them a deck of cards and an instruction sheet.
    Instruction sheets are available on the Pinterest board. Have students
    arrange the cards according to the instruction sheet. Write on the
    board: Which way is the best way to put the cards in categories? How
    do you know? Next, one member of each group shares their categories,
    processes, and thinking.

2. For the next activity, have students return to their groups. Provide
    each group with a grab-bag of 15–20 random items, such as scissors,
    a piece of ribbon, five paper clips, a rock, etc. Have students take
    the objects out of the bags. Explain that their task is to create three
    collections from the items.

    • Observe 2 minutes of silence for thinking time. Starting with the
      person who has a birthday closest to today, each group member
      should share her or his ideas for the collections. All group members
      collaborate to create the group's three collections.

    • Each group shares how they arranged the items with the
      entire class.

3. For the final activity, students move around to show their choices. First, have the students stand up away from any table or desk. Explain that they are going to show their decisions by moving to different locations. Give the choices and provide time for them to move.

- Which do you like most? Cats or dogs? Point to different sides of the room.
- What is your favorite breakfast? Cereal or eggs?
- Which is your favorite ice cream flavor? Vanilla? Chocolate? Strawberry?
- What is your favorite food? Do not give any choices for this one. Let them figure out groups by themselves.
- What is your favorite thing to do on the weekends?

4. Debrief using whole-class discussion. Sit in a circle. Use the Marker Mic strategy. Pose the questions below and hand the Marker Mic to a student.

- Which were easier to answer?
- When did you learn more?

5. Explain to students that they were creating categories, an important part of learning to curate.

6. Engage students in written reflection and discussion.

- Remind students about both of the activities.
- Write the phrase on the board: Categories are . . .
- Students free-write in journals or paper for 5 minutes.
- Students reread and underline sentences that capture their ideas the best.
- Provide time for them to share their writing, either by reading it aloud or by having them rewrite what they wrote and posting it on a bulletin board.

TECH UPGRADE FOR THIS LESSON

The writing could be done in Google Docs and shared with the class. Students could look for connections between their understanding and that of their classmates.

ARE THEY GETTING IT? POTENTIAL MISCONCEPTIONS AND SNAGS

Some students may find it challenging to build categories from the items in the bag. You could make the groupings more apparent: Have all red and green items or different sized items. For the moving around activity, allow students to explain their choices to make the development of the categories clearer.

LESSON 3: CREATING NEW FROM OLD

This lesson focuses on students creating from ideas that they provide to each other. Curating is about identifying the important information and then blending it together to make something new. Student will share ideas together and then write a story based on the ideas they gather from their small group.

GENERAL PROCEDURES

1. Divide the class into groups of three and give each member of the group a number, *1* to *3*. All of the number *1*s stand at the front of the classroom. Numbers *2* and *3* stand at the back. Hand the *1*s an envelope with an image in it. The *1*s study the image for a minute and return it to the envelope. The *2*s then come to the front of the classroom, and the *1*s quietly describe the image that they saw to their teammate. When they are done with the description, the *2*s write down what they were told. When the *2*s finish writing down the description, they take the description back to the *3*s, who read it and then draw the image as described in the writing. Each group shares their final drawing and notes similarities and differences across the class. Whole-group discussion is used as needed to explain the process that creates new ideas from old ones (Sprenger, 2003).

SUPER TIP

INCLUDING REGULAR OPPORTUNITIES FOR MOVEMENT IS CRITICAL. A STUDENT'S ATTENTION SPAN USUALLY LASTS FOR ABOUT 10 MINUTES.

2. Arrange the class into groups of four. Give each group a series of 10–15 words from across your curriculum. These words may or may not be on the same topic.

3. Each member of the group creates their own "personal library" of categories from the words.

4. Tell the students that they are going to be writing a story using the words and categories that they generated. Students have to use at least 10 words in their story.

5. To prepare for their writing, take a Silent Walk to think about their story. They may take their papers along on the walk. Explain the rules of a Silent Walk:

   - It must be silent the entire time.
   - It is a time for thinking.

- Students walk in a line and avoid eye contact with their peers.
- When the walk is over, it is still Silent Time!

6. Take the walk. It should last around 5 minutes. It needs to be long enough for students to adjust to the activity and have time to think.

7. After returning to the classroom, give at least 30 minutes for the students to write a story, using their categories and words.

8. If students finish ahead of the others, have them make illustrations for their stories or read from classroom texts to search for the words.

9. Whisper-read as a means of proofreading and editing. Have the students spread themselves out around the classroom and in the hall, if possible. Explain to them that they need to actually be able to hear themselves reading the story. Walk around to verify that they are actually whispering.

10. Sitting in their groups, students read their stories to each other. Each student first identifies which words he or she used in the story. Students raise a finger if they also used that word, and the story reader keeps track of how many used the same word as they did. Discuss similarities and differences among the stories.

TECH UPGRADE FOR THIS LESSON

A fun way to follow connections is to see where a student's interest will take them. Have them go to URoulette.com. It generates random sites. Choose your favorite number. Go to that number on the list. Click on any link in the website that comes up. Go to the next link. Repeat this five to six times and see where the links take you. It is a means of recognizing that other people have interests and curiosity about topics that also interest you.

ARE THEY GETTING IT? POTENTIAL MISCONCEPTIONS AND SNAGS

Students for whom writing is a challenge could record their stories and play them back or they could share them with the teacher. Students could also draw illustrations to communicate their ideas.

FORMATIVE ASSESSMENT AND TRACKING STUDENT PROGRESS TOWARD GOALS

At the end of each lesson, students should self-assess their progress using the arrow continuum related to each journey goal using a yellow crayon. (See the following Formative Tracking Sheet for the arrow continuum.) You may also wish to have students provide notes or evidence justifying their rating. After students self-evaluate, you should assess their progress using a blue crayon. In every case where your rating agrees with the student's rating, it will create a "green light." This helps students to norm their ability to track their own progress. After using this strategy for some time, you'll likely find that most students are more stringent on their performance than you are!

Not only does this twofold method give you helpful information for future lessons, but it is also a strategy that significantly accelerates student achievement (Hattie, 2009). Go to the Pinterest page for this instructional journey to download the tracking sheet.

FINAL ASSESSMENT: HAVE YOUR GOALS BEEN ACHIEVED?

CREATING SCHOOL CLUBS

For the final assessment of this unit, students will identify, categorize, and synthesize information from their peers and the community. The school principal will be the authentic audience for this task. Using Marc Prensky's definition of passion, "things you like to spend your time on when no one is making you do something else," students will advise the principal on the creation of three school clubs (Prensky, 2010, p. 55).

STUDENT-FRIENDLY PROMPT

The time has arrived! Your school is going to create new clubs for students. Your principal has asked you to research and curate the passions in your class and community so that he or she can figure out which three clubs are worth supporting. You can include the interests of parents, peers, and teachers. Now it is time to get started!

This will be a time of learning independently and collaboratively.

First we are each going to share what our passions are and see if there are others with similar or very different passions in our class or community. Also, I have arranged for a number of adults to share with you from around the school and from around the world. They will visit in person or via Skype to tell us about their passions, share their experiences, and suggest club activities.

Working in groups of three, you must figure out how to organize, prioritize, and categorize this information for your principal.

At the end of the lesson, you will create a 3-minute "elevator speech," to share with your principal about the three clubs she or he should create using evidence from your research.

FORMATIVE TRACKING SHEET: SOLVING A PUZZLE

Formative Tracking Sheet: Solving a Puzzle

How do you curate? How do I make sense out of all of the information in the world? How do I save and organize the information that I find? How do I create something new from all that I find? How do I share my thinking?

Unit Goals:

GOAL 1:	GOAL 2:	GOAL 3:
Recognize important information.	Categorize.	Synthesize many different sources.

Learning Target for Goal 1: I can recognize important information.

Lesson 1:
Lesson Task: Identify words.

Lesson 1:
Lesson Task: Identify images.

Lesson 1:
Lesson Task: Identify sounds.

Lesson 1:
Lesson Task: Whole-group debrief at the lesson's end.

Rate your own mastery of this learning target after each lesson. Remember that your rating can change over time:

New to Me ⟵——————————————⟶ I Got This!

Learning Target for Goal 2: I can build categories.

Lesson 2:
Lesson Task: Dividing cards and organizing collections.

Lesson 3:
Lesson Task: Creating categories from words.

Rate your own mastery of this learning target. Remember that your rating can change over time:

New to Me ⟵——————————————⟶ I Got This!

Learning Target for Goal 3: I can blend and share my new ideas.

Lesson 3:
Lesson Task: Drawing pictures with teams.

Lesson 3:
Lesson Task: Writing a new story from categories and words.

Rate your own mastery of this learning target. Remember that your rating can change over time:

New to Me ⟵——————————————⟶ I Got This!

SOURCE: This tool was inspired by a tool shared by Bill Ferriter in a blog post: http://blog.williamferriter.com/2013/02/16/my-middle-schoolers-actually-love-our-unit-overview-sheets

RUBRIC INDICATOR	SUPERHERO	SIDEKICK	APPRENTICE
Recognizing	You recognized what needed to be found and stayed focused until you were able to find it.	You worked hard most of the time to find what needed to be found.	You looked for each item, but sometimes became distracted.
Categorizing	You recognized which items belonged together and built clear categories.	You saw some patterns among the objects and made connections between them.	You began to put some items together to make connections, but left many without a group.
Making New From Old	You blended together ideas and items to create a new idea.	You found some aspects of different ideas that you connected with each other, but you need to include more.	You were focused on one idea and had trouble adding to it to make something new.

DIFFERENTIATION: MEETING THE NEEDS OF ALL LEARNERS

The lessons to develop the Curating Superpower can be expanded or contracted to meet the needs of a wide variety of learners. For the reading activities, such as the Words on a Page station, a variety of reading levels can be used. Allow students to choose whichever ones they want to do: above grade level, at grade, and below. Below are a few specific suggestions to adjust this instructional journey:

- Choose Hidden Pictures that are more apparent or more hidden to decrease or increase the difficulty.

- Teach a lesson on listening to music. Have the students place one hand in front of their chest. Play the music. Have them raise a finger when they hear the sound for which they are listening. This gives privacy during the learning stage. Have music where the sounds are more or less apparent.

- The collection of items in the bag could have more apparent categories.

- Students can be given choices in how they express what they learned about categories. They could talk about it with the teacher or make drawings to show their understanding.

- Depending on the ability or grade level, the amount and type of work can be varied. It can range from all drawings with short captions to extended writing.

WINDOW INTO THE CLASSROOM

Ben is a teacher in a fourth-grade classroom in the suburbs, outside a large city. He has a class of 25 students and wants to encourage them to take more control over their own learning. Many of his students have access to a computer and seem to be aware of the wealth of information that is available to them simply by doing a Google search. Ben wants to help them learn the tools to organize and use the information that surrounds them. He realized that through this instructional journey, he could teach the skills without having the students on laptops. For young learners, beginning with a kinesthetic activity before moving to a digital environment can be helpful. Ben's goal was to make the necessary connections during the work so that students would be able to transfer skills to the digital world.

When Ben introduced the Curating Superpower to his class, his students were excited. Ben explained that the first skill that they needed to learn was observation. He told them that they already had some good skills, but that they were going to continue to hone them. He described each station and told them that they had 45 minutes to move between the four stations. They needed to go to each one, but they could decide how long they wanted to stay there.

At the end of the time, students wrote an Exit Card to help them gather their thoughts about what they had learned about observing. What was fun about it? What works well? What was challenging? Although this activity wasn't in the lesson activity, Ben felt that it was important for students to capture their ideas in writing.

Ben then divided the group into partners, with one group of three. They shared their ideas about observing and using markers and big paper, creating a poster with the title, "Tips for Great Observing." When the students finished their posters, Ben hung them up in the hallway outside his classroom. The posters advised such things as: "Observing works best when you pay attention," "Don't look around the room when you are observing," and "You can learn a lot of details when you observe."

Ben decided to divide the "Where Does It Go?" lesson and do it over three days. He wanted to make sure that he kept the students' attention through each activity. The groups for dividing the decks of cards quickly accomplished the task and eagerly began to write in response to guiding questions that Ben wrote on the board. Which way is the best way to put the cards in categories? How do you know? After 5 minutes of writing, Ben had some students share what they had written. Ben collected their writing to assess later.

With the bag challenge and the moving around challenge, Ben helped the students realize that the categories that they chose made a big difference. Sometimes broad categories were useful, and sometimes narrower ones were needed.

Before beginning the last lesson, Ben met with his principal to verify that it was okay for him to take his students for the Silent Walk. It wasn't something that Ben had ever tried before or ever heard of teachers doing, and he wanted to make sure that he had permission. While the principal was a bit wary, he decided to give Ben a chance to try it out. Ben made sure that the class was aware that this was a privilege and that they needed to carefully follow the rules. Ben lined them up and off they went. The results, both during the walk and then the writing time, were amazing. The students were focused and engaged the entire time.

When they shared their writing, it was clear that they loved the novelty of the experience as well as the result. They saw the significance of their own thinking as they shared and listened to their classmates. They understood that they each had the power to create a unique concept or story based on their ways of thinking. They all started in the same place but ended up with wildly different ideas.

The students brought all of their curating skills to bear for the final assessment. Two parents came in to share their passions with the students: fly-fishing and painting. They each brought in equipment that they used and photographs of themselves as they did it. Ben hung up the images of favorite streams and of favorite paintings on the wall.

Then, students in the class shared their interests with each other and filled in the Personal Passion sheets. Ben hung the sheets up, and students left sticky notes on each other's Passion sheets.

Finally, Ben had a friend who was a chef at a restaurant, and since many of the students were interested in food in one way or another, he had her Skype in, using her phone to give a tour of the kitchen and restaurant. She very willingly answered questions and shared her experiences.

Working in groups of three, the students generated a list of questions to help them identify what kinds of clubs other students might be interested having at the school. They created interview sheets from the lists. They met with other students, teachers, and members of the community, gathering the necessary evidence.

The students created charts to record the responses from their interviews, identifying the most desired clubs. Each student then chose the three clubs that he or she wanted to present in an "elevator speech." The students wrote and practiced their speeches before presenting them to the principal.

The students had learned to find important information, build categories, and blend together what they had learned, share, and make connections. They had curating superpowers!

● ●

A QUESTION TO CONSIDER AS YOU REFLECT

- Where do you see opportunities for curation as a way of making meaning in every subject area?

THE CONNECTING INSTRUCTIONAL JOURNEY

SHARING STORIES

SUPERPOWER SUMMARY AND OVERVIEW

In the world of instant global interactions, students must have the tools to effectively communicate and connect with people both in the same room and around the world. They are, as Marc Prensky has labeled them, "digital natives," having been born into a world that includes not only the Internet but microchips in almost every place they look. The Connecting Superpower provides them with the tools to share their ideas clearly and to listen to the thinking of others. It helps them to communicate and collaborate to reach whatever the goal may be.

Humans have connected to one another throughout history by telling stories. They pass on their experiences, share their wisdom, and learn together through their stories. In his book *A Whole New Mind*, Daniel Pink (2006) devotes a chapter to story, calling it "the ability to encapsulate, contextualize and emotionalize." It is critical for students to practice telling their story. They need to learn to identify what is significant in their story and articulate it to others in ways that effectively build connections. They then need to know how to listen closely to the stories of others. The Connecting Superpower teaches them to do both.

CONNECTING JOURNEY AT A GLANCE

SHARING STORIES

Instructional Journey Goals	1. Articulate clearly in speech and writing. 2. Develop effective questions for interview. 3. Empathize.

General Progression	→ Communicate clearly.
	    → Listen carefully.
	        → Empathize and make connections with others.

Connecting the Standards	Common Core State Standards for Reading, Writing, and Speaking and Listening • W.4—FOCUS STANDARD • W.6—FOCUS STANDARD • W.5 • R.10 • SL.1 • SL.2 • SL.3 National Curriculum Standards for Social Studies • Culture • People, Places, and Environment • Individual Development and Identity Common Core State Standards of Math Practice • SMP 1
Learning Activities	Lesson 1: Who Am I? Lesson 2: So Who Are You? Lesson 3: Let's Walk Together Lesson 4: Creating a Digital You
Tech Upgrades	• Doppleme—www.doppelme.com • Comic Life—http://comiclife.com • Kidblogs—www.kidblogs.com
Final Assessment	Connecting Around the World

Howard Rheingold, in his book *Netsmart,* advocates for developing student skills about building communities and connections. Rheingold (2012) states,

> What matters the most with present-day new literacies are not just the encoding and decoding skills an individual needs to know to join the community of literates but also the ability to use those skills socially, in concert with others, in an effective way. (p. 4)

To do this, teachers need to start with themselves. They need to evaluate their ability to respect and connect with those different from themselves. Teachers need to focus on helping students understand their feelings as well as their ideas and prepare them to share these ideas with each other.

INSTRUCTIONAL JOURNEY GOALS

1. Articulate clearly in speech and writing.
2. Develop effective questions for interview.
3. Empathize.

STUDENT-FRIENDLY AUTHENTIC LEARNING PROBLEM

What is your story? How can you tell it? Imagine having friends around the world who are sharing stories and interests! What does it take to make those connections and build an online community?

GENERAL PROGRESSION

→ Communicate clearly.
  → Listen carefully.
    → Empathize and make connections with others.

CONNECTING THE STANDARDS

As this instructional journey and superpower are closely linked to critical literacy, the two focus standards come from the ELA Common Core. Areas that show increasing complexity are underlined for your reference (see the following table).

OVERALL STANDARD	GRADE 3	GRADE 4	GRADE 5
W.4: Produce clear and coherent writing in which the development, organization, and style are appropriate to task, purpose, and audience.	**W.4.3:** With guidance and support from adults, produce writing in which the development and organization are appropriate to task and purpose.	**W.4.4:** With guidance and support from adults, produce writing in which the development and organization are appropriate to task and purpose.	**W.4.5:** With guidance and support from adults, produce writing in which the development and organization are appropriate to task and purpose.
W.6: Use technology, including the Internet, to produce and publish writing and to interact and collaborate with others.	**W.6.3:** With guidance and support from adults, use technology to produce and publish writing (using keyboarding skills) as well as to interact and collaborate with others.	**W.6.4:** With some guidance and support from adults, use technology, including the Internet, to produce and publish writing as well as to interact and collaborate with others; demonstrate sufficient command of keyboarding skills to type a minimum of one page in a single sitting.	**W.6.5:** With some guidance and support from adults, use technology, including the Internet, to produce and publish writing as well as to interact and collaborate with others; demonstrate sufficient command of keyboarding skills to type a minimum of two pages in a single sitting.

CONNECTIONS TO OTHER STANDARDS

COMMON CORE STATE STANDARDS FOR
READING, WRITING, AND SPEAKING AND LISTENING

- **R.10**—Read and comprehend literary and informational texts independently and proficiently.
- **W.5**—Develop and strengthen writing as needed by planning, revising, editing, rewriting, or trying a new approach.
- **SL.1**—Prepare for and participate effectively in a range of conversations and collaborations with diverse partners, building on others' ideas and expressing their own clearly and persuasively.
- **SL.2**—Integrate and evaluate information presented in diverse media and formats, including visually, quantitatively, and orally.

- **SL.3**—Evaluate a speaker's point of view, reasoning and use of evidence and rhetoric.

NATIONAL CURRICULUM STANDARDS FOR SOCIAL STUDIES

- Culture
- People, Place, Environments
- Individual Development and Identity

COMMON CORE STATE STANDARDS OF MATH PRACTICE

- **SMP 1**—Make sense of problems and persevere in solving them.

LEARNING ACTIVITIES AND TECH UPGRADES

There are four lessons associated with this journey. In this book, lessons are defined as related series of student-driven explorations, not merely what will fit in a single class period. Actually, it is likely that each of these lessons will take several class periods to complete. After students explore all four lessons, provide them with the transfer task that follows to obtain summative data relative to the journey goals. All lesson resources (labeled for easy use) can be found on this Pinterest board:

http://pinterest.com/ssuperpowers/connecting-journey

(You can follow all Student Superpower Pinterest boards at **http://pinterest.com/ssuperpowers/boards**.)

LESSON 1: WHO AM I?

This lesson focuses on helping students tell personal stories. It is important when developing the Connecting Superpower to understand oneself and be able to talk about individual emotions and experiences in a way that connects with others.

1. Explain that connecting with other people starts with knowing oneself and telling one's story. The teacher brings in a collection of items from his or her personal life to share with the class: baby picture, school report card, souvenir from a trip. Share aspects of yourself that you wouldn't normally in a standard classroom environment. Focus on how each person is unique, with different likes, dislikes, strengths, and challenges. End the story by listing emotions related to the personal story.

2. Have students create a display of emotion words. Ask students, "What words can we put on our wall to tell our stories and about how we feel? What are some different emotions that we have?" Have

students use index cards to put emotion words on the wall: *happy, sad, scared, excited, worried*. This wall will be called the Sharing Stories Wall.

3. Review each word on the wall. Have students make faces or simple skits to illustrate each one.

4. Read Dr. Seuss' *My Many Colored Days*. (More information is available on the Pinterest board for this journey.)

   - Hand out markers and white paper.
   - Have students choose four colors. Have them create one cartoon for each color that illustrates their feelings or a story from their life as they connect with that color.
   - Hang them on the Sharing Stories wall.

5. Give students homework to prepare for Lesson 2: Bring in five items that are significant to you. Place items in a brown paper bag.

TECH UPGRADE FOR THIS LESSON

Students could take photographs of each other making the various faces to add to the Sharing Stories Wall. Students could create a collection of avatars to illustrate a variety of emotions, using a tool like Doppleme.com. This could put some distance between them and their emotions, which could allow them to discuss more difficult feelings.

ARE THEY GETTING IT? POTENTIAL MISCONCEPTIONS AND SNAGS

One goal of this lesson is to begin to develop language to talk about feelings and to be able to present their story. Make sure that there are a wide variety of words on the Sharing Stories Wall. If necessary, add some words to it. Also, try to avoid students wanting to create the perfect drawing during the activity with *My Many Colored Days*. Review the images in *My Many Colored Days* and remind students that the goal is for them to think about themselves and their stories.

LESSON 2: SO WHO ARE YOU?

For this lesson, students work in groups of four. Students share the items in their bag with group members, looking for similarities and differences. They then divide into pairs and interview each other, creating nametags for their partner. Students will build the nametag out of a wide variety of materials, using it as a means to present what they learned about the person they interviewed.

GENERAL PROCEDURES

1. The teacher creates groups of four. Students sit together with the brown bags that they brought in. Explain that the goal is for each

student to share what they brought, explaining its significance. Starting with the person with the birthday closest to the day, have them present what they brought.

2. Introduce the process of conducting interviews to learn more about one of their classmates.

3. Ask the students to write questions that would help someone conduct a successful interview to learn about what is important about that person and their story. What would they need to ask to learn interesting information about a person?

4. Sitting in a circle, have each student share one question they created or choose one that another student shared. Students can add questions to their own lists.

5. Have the students return to their groups of four. Have them choose a number between 1 and 4. Pair up *1*s and *3*s, and *2*s and *4*s, to interview each other.

6. Taking turns, have the students interview each other and record the information that they learned. Each interview should last 5 minutes. They should not switch until the 5 minutes is over. They may ask follow-up questions.

7. Next, students create a 3D nametag for the person that they interviewed. Introduce any materials that are available: 5" × 7" index cards, markers, colored paper, pipe cleaners, and other interesting items.

8. Separate the students into two groups: *1*s and *2*s are together; *3*s and *4*s are together. Students should be building the nametags with peers that they did *not* interview. These are their Building Groups. Build for at least 30 minutes. Play music while they are working.

9. All students come together and exchange nametags.

10. Nametag Fashion Show: Have students sit along the hallway on both sides with the person who made their nametag. Have each pair stand. While one "walks the runway," have the other explain why they created the nametag the way that they did.

11. Students write a reflection on one of the following topics:

    - Does the nametag work for them? Why or why not?
    - What should be changed about their nametag? Why?
    - Why are good questions important?

TECH UPGRADE FOR THIS LESSON

The interviews could be done using Google Forms if the students are not in the same classroom. The nametags should not be made digitally. It is an important part of the process to have them actually build them (Martinez & Stager, 2013).

ARE THEY GETTING IT? POTENTIAL MISCONCEPTIONS AND SNAGS

It can be difficult for students to share their stories. Arrange the groups carefully to make sure that students are paired with sympathetic partners. Also, some students struggle with the building process. Remind them that the goal is not a perfectly constructed nametag, but one that communicates about the person for whom they are creating it.

LESSON 3: LET'S WALK TOGETHER

This lesson is to help students identify the similarities and differences that they have with each other. It helps them to listen carefully and empathize with others. It deepens the skills practiced in the second lesson.

GENERAL PROCEDURES

1. What is empathy?

   - Watch the *Sesame Street* video on empathy. It is available on the Pinterest board for this journey.

   - Pose the question: What is empathy?

   - In groups of three, have students brainstorm a list of words that describe the word *empathy*. Allow the students to spread out around the room to do this.

   - Have them write their definition on a piece of paper and create an illustration to go with it.

   - Have the class sit in a circle and share their definitions.

   - Develop a class definition for empathy. Write it on paper to hang on the Sharing Stories Wall.

   - Pose the question: How does our definition connect with the statement on the board?

2. Organize students into pairs. Give each pair a set of emotion cards that include the following words: *happy, sad, excited, scared, angry.* These are downloadable on the Pinterest board for this journey.

   - Give students 2 minutes of quiet to think about a time when they felt this emotion. Students draw a stick figure cartoon to connect with the experience and write the word underneath it.

   - All partners share their cartoon.

   - Repeat this process for all five cards.

   - Students hang their cartoons on the Sharing Stories Wall.

SUPER TIP

ENCOURAGING EMPATHY IN THE CLASSROOM
BETTER PREPARES STUDENTS TO FACE
INTERDEPENDENT, GLOBAL, 21ST CENTURY TASKS.

4. Have a whole-class debrief on the experience. Ask students to reflect on how different people experience the same emotions.

5. Next, choose one or both of the following activities to allow students to think about the experiences and feelings of a person they don't know.

6. How Does It Feel? Fairy Tale

   • Read *The True Story of the Three Little Pigs* by Jon Scieszka. Discuss what "point of view" is. More information about this resource is available on the Pinterest board for this journey.

   • Have students choose another fairy tale or animated movie, for example:

     o Jack and the Beanstalk—giant

     o Cinderella—one of the ugly stepsisters

     o *The Lion King*—Uncle Scar

   • Create a four-frame cartoon from the villain's point of view.

7. How Does It Feel? History

   • Gather a collection of primary source photographs, connected with the Social Studies curriculum. The Library of Congress is a wonderful resource for these images, and a direct link is available on the Pinterest board for this journey.

   • Write the following questions on the board:

     o What do you see? What details do you notice?

     o What do you think?

     o What do you wonder?

   • Have the students write a mini-saga, no more than 50 words, from the perspective of the person in the photograph (Pink, 2006, p. 119).

TECH UPGRADE FOR THIS LESSON

Comic Life could be used to make the cartoons. The Library of Congress has an online tool to facilitate analyzing primary sources that helps students ask and answer the appropriate questions of each kind of source. A direct link to the tool is available on the Pinterest board for this journey.

ARE THEY GETTING IT? POTENTIAL MISCONCEPTIONS AND SNAGS

If students have trouble talking about themselves, they can create a fictional character or talk about a character in a book or movie with whom they are familiar. Remind the students to use the Sharing Feelings Wall to generate ideas and find the words to help them express themselves.

LESSON 4: CREATING A DIGITAL YOU

In this lesson, students will recognize their visibility while online and develop a personal profile that allows them to be known but still safe. They will use the format of blogging to write their responses to questions posed both by the teacher and fellow students. They will write comments on each other's posts as a means of practicing digital connections, an important aspect of the Connecting Superpower. If available, they will use a digital tool, such as KidBlogs.com, to do this writing.

GENERAL PROCEDURES

1. Have a student review the class definition of empathy.

2. Pose the question: What do you need to know to have empathy? Give 2–3 minutes of quiet for writing a list. Have the students share them with their partner.

3. Have them all go to the board and write down the top three items on their list.

4. In pairs, have the students play the children's game peekaboo with each other, first one, then the other, then at the same time. Have them discuss what happens when you play peekaboo.

5. Have these questions written on cards. Hand one to a student. Have them read it aloud and call on other students to answer. Write answers on the board:

   - What is the connection between playing peekaboo and being online?
   - Why are seeing and being seen important when making connections?
   - What can I share about myself and still be safe?
   - What shouldn't I share?

SUPER TIP

PROVIDING EXPLICIT INSTRUCTION ON HOW TO BE SAFE ONLINE IS NEEDED IN ALL SUBJECT AREAS.

6. Write "Share" and "Don't Share" on the board. Record student responses.

7. Hand out the Profile Worksheet and have students create a profile for themselves. Remind them that the goal is to be "Seen and Safe." The Profile Worksheet is downloadable on the Pinterest board for this unit.

8. Hang the profiles. Give out red and blue dots or markers to each student. Have them read each other's profiles and identify good information to share (blue) and bad information to share (red).

9. Hand out the Blog Post worksheet that is available for download on the Pinterest board for this journey. Explain that each student is going to write a blog post that will be public and hung in the hallway for the members of the school community to see, people that they do not necessarily know. Tell them that the community is going to be asked to leave comments on the blog posts. They can choose any topic that they want for their writing. It just needs to be authentic. Give them 3–5 minutes of quiet to think, no writing allowed. Then provide writing time.

10. Collect the blog posts. Read and give feedback on the following: appropriate information to share, spelling and grammar, incomplete thoughts.

11. Have students rewrite blog posts and hang them in the hallway with Comment sheets below them. Invite the school community to comment.

12. Explain to students and the school community that comments are for developing a conversation. Introduce Rules for Commenting:

    - Never write your last name.
    - Write in complete sentences.
    - Avoid simply saying, "Great!" or "I agree." Explain why.
    - Remember this is the start of a conversation between you and the author of the blog.

13. Tell the students that they have 30 minutes now to read and comment on each other's blogs, but that the blogs will stay up for the week.

TECH UPGRADE FOR THIS LESSON

While this can be done online, it is better to start students with blogging offline. It makes the process and its visibility more apparent to them.

ARE THEY GETTING IT? POTENTIAL MISCONCEPTIONS AND SNAGS

If students are uncomfortable with hanging their blog posts in the hallway, use the classroom walls instead. They can work in small groups, reading their blog posts and giving feedback to one another. The first round of leaving comments could be done with sticky notes. Then there could be a lesson on effective comments.

FORMATIVE ASSESSMENT AND TRACKING STUDENT PROGRESS TOWARD GOALS

At the end of each lesson, students should self-assess their progress using the arrow continuum related to each journey goal using a yellow crayon. (See the following Formative Tracking Sheet for the arrow continuum.) You may also wish to have students provide notes or evidence justifying their rating. After students self-evaluate, you should assess their progress using a blue crayon. In every case where your rating agrees with the student's rating, it will create a "green light." This helps students to norm their ability to track their own progress. After using this strategy for some time, you'll likely find that most students are more stringent on their performance than you are!

Not only does this twofold method give you helpful information for future lessons, but it is also a strategy that significantly accelerates student achievement (Hattie, 2009). Go to the Pinterest page for this instructional journey to download the tracking sheet.

FINAL ASSESSMENT: HAVE YOUR GOALS BEEN ACHIEVED?

CONNECTING AROUND THE WORLD

The final assessment is to safely connect students with other people around the world and to let them practice the skills they have been building. They will be listening, asking questions, investigating, and sharing. Parts of the assessment are built around connections through Skype in the Classroom, a wonderful resource for teachers. A direct link to this resource is available on the Pinterest board for this journey. Students will join a KidBlog classroom. They will blog and comment on each other's writing. They will make connections with students in other classrooms.

STUDENT-FRIENDLY PROMPT

Today we are going to have a Mystery Skype call to another classroom somewhere in the world. I have contacted teachers who are interested in playing with us from a list of teachers who want to connect via Mystery Skype. (See the Pinterest board for this journey for the list. Special thanks

FORMATIVE TRACKING SHEET: SHARING STORIES

Formative Tracking Sheet: Sharing Stories

How do you connect? How do I share who I am with other people? How do I listen and learn from others? How do I have empathy for others? How can I make the world a better place?

Unit Goals:

GOAL 1:
☑ Articulate clearly in speech and writing.

GOAL 2:
☑ Develop effective questions for interview.

GOAL 3:
☑ Empathize.

Learning Target for Goal 1: I can share my ideas.

Lesson 1:
Lesson Task: I can illustrate a wide range of emotions.

Lesson 3:
Lesson Task: I shared my own stories.

Lesson 4:
Lesson Task: I shared my own stories.

Rate your own mastery of this learning target after each lesson. Remember that your rating can change over time:

New to Me ◄————————————————► I Got This!

Learning Target for Goal 2: I can develop and ask effective questions.

Lesson 2:
Lesson Task: I asked good questions.
Lesson Task: I listened carefully to the answers.

Lesson 3:
Lesson Task: I respect other points of view.
Lesson Task: I recognized similarities and differences between my categories and those of my partners.

Rate your own mastery of this learning target. Remember that your rating can change over time:

New to Me ◄————————————————► I Got This!

Learning Target for Goal 3: I act with empathy for others.

Lesson 2:
Lesson Task: I understood the feelings expressed by my partner.
Lesson Task: I made a nametag that showed the person's personality.

Lesson 3:
Lesson Task: I was able to understand another point of view.

Lesson 4:
Lesson Task: I made connections by writing effective comments.

Rate your own mastery of this learning target. Remember that your rating can change over time:

New to Me ◄————————————————► I Got This!

SOURCE: This tool was inspired by a tool shared by Bill Ferriter in a blog post:
http://blog.williamferriter.com/2013/02/16/my-middle-schoolers-actually-love-our-unit-overview-sheets

to Paula Naugle, @plnaugle, for creating the list!) I am not going to tell you where they are and they are not going to know where you are. It will be your job, and the job of the other class, to guess where each classroom is. We are going to visit one classroom that is in the United States and one that is not.

You first need to develop a list of questions that we can ask to help us figure out where they are. You may only ask questions that have "Yes" or "No" for the answer. With a partner, you will write as many questions as you can think of that will help us locate them. Look at the map of the world and the map of the United States to help you develop your questions. We will all share our questions and decide which ones we want to ask first.

Then it will be time to make the calls. We are going to do one call today and another tomorrow. Once the calls are finished, I will invite the students from the other classroom to share in our Kidblogs classroom. You will each write a blog post. Once you are ready to post your writing, you will edit another student's work, helping him or her to make it clear and interesting. After all of the writing has been edited, we will post them on Kidblogs.

Finally, it will be time to read and comment on the stories and ideas of other students, both in your classroom and in the other two classrooms with which you connected.

STUDENT-FRIENDLY RUBRIC

RUBRIC INDICATOR	SUPERHERO	SIDEKICK	APPRENTICE
Share Honestly	You understand yourself and can share your feelings and ideas clearly.	You are more comfortable talking about some things than others.	You find it challenging to talk about yourself.
Empathize	You listen very well to others and find many ways to understand their experiences.	You listen well and try to find ways to understand others.	You sometimes interrupt people while they are sharing their stories.
Make Connections	You communicate well and look for ways to build relationships with others.	You try to find links between your life and other people's, but sometimes it is difficult.	You stumble upon connections more than seek them.

DIFFERENTIATION: MEETING THE NEEDS OF ALL LEARNERS

This journey can be easily adapted to meet the needs of individual students. There are many stories for students that present different emotions. There are also many children's books that discuss family challenges and emotions that could be read aloud to the class. Below are a few specific suggestions to adjust this journey:

- Each lesson could be adapted to include more writing components. For the first part of the lesson, the students could write about themselves and explain the connection between themselves and what they placed in the bag. They could also write an explanation of why they created the nametag in the fashion that they did.

- The empathy lesson could be simplified by having the teacher generate the questions for the interview process or by having the class as a whole generate them.

- You can watch *"Sesame Street:* Elmo's Interview on YouTube" to understand the interview process and interesting questions to ask. This video is available on the Pinterest board for this journey.

- Students could write out one or more of the stories that they shared in the "What is empathy?" activity. They could also create full cartoons to show their story.

- If students are having trouble deciding on a topic to write about, provide some suggestions.

- Challenge the students to bring about change in the world! Read about how Bill Ferriter used Kiva to expand his students' understanding of the world and to make a difference in the lives of others. A direct link to this post is available on the Pinterest board for this journey.

- When connecting with some classrooms where the students must walk great distances to attend school, have the students take a long walk (1–2 miles) to develop empathy for the students with whom they will be speaking.

WINDOW INTO THE CLASSROOM

Maria teaches in a fourth-grade classroom in an urban school. She is a relatively new teacher with a class of 24 students. She is very eager to empower her students and help them connect with the world beyond their neighborhood. Maria created the Sharing Stories Wall by putting newspapers on her main bulletin board, hoping to make the connection between professional writing and her students' work. She thought carefully about what to bring in to start the unit. She wanted to make her story real for them. She finally chose a baby picture, an old report card, program from a concert in which her choir sang, and a movie ticket. She hung them beside the Sharing Stories Wall.

Lesson 1 caught the students' imagination. They loved hearing Maria's story, laughing at her baby picture, and finding the comments on her report card. Maria often started a unit with a Vocabulary Wall, to access any prior knowledge, so her students quickly started writing when she gave the prompt, generating a wall of words and giggling as they made faces for each one. The *Many Colored Days* activity gave them a chance to think about themselves and work with the new vocabulary, as they each wrote a caption for their drawings. She gave them the homework of bringing in five items to share their story for the next day's class.

Maria decided to show the first 10 minutes of the Elmo interview video as a hook at the beginning of Lesson 2. She then divided them into groups of four to share what they had brought in. Maria made sure not to rush them as they told their stories and looked for similarities among them. When it came time to write a list of questions, they were ready to go. They conducted the interviews, incredibly eager to create the 3D nametags. They colored, stapled, folded, and glued while tapping their feet to the jazz playing in the background.

The conversation that followed the exchange was lively and informative, with students recognizing themselves in the nametags. But, they also realized that there were aspects that had been left out or that had been misinterpreted. They had to work as a team to correct misconceptions. Maria and the students were aware of the sense of community that was developing among them.

The empathy lesson grew naturally out of the previous one, with students sharing their experiences and listening to the stories of their partners. Maria chose to do the fairy tale "So How Does It Feel?" She read the story and handed out 11" × 17" paper. She gave the students three options, but said that they could do any fairy tale that they wanted. The Uncle Scar from *The Lion King* proved to be a favorite.

Playing peekaboo was the hit of the fourth lesson, combining laughter and fun while communicating that they are always visible. It helped the students to understand that anything that they post online can be seen and becomes part of them. They successfully built their profiles, communicating good information about themselves to help make connections. Because they had been telling so many stories about themselves over the course of the earlier lessons, the students easily chose a topic for their blog post. The earlier conversations had also prepared them for writing effective comments in each other's blogs. They could make connections between the stories of their peers and their own, clearly practicing empathy.

For the final assessment, Maria connected with two classrooms, one in Alaska and another in New Zealand via the Mystery Skype Website. She invited the teachers to share the Kidblogs class after the calls were completed. The calls were amazingly successful, engaging the students and encouraging them to write and share with students around the world. The students began to regularly share blog posts, eager to connect with a real audience.

● ●

A QUESTION TO CONSIDER AS YOU REFLECT

- How can we build connections for our students in school, their city, and around the world?

THE DIGITAL INKING INSTRUCTIONAL JOURNEY

WHAT SHOULD WE TWEET?

SUPERPOWER SUMMARY AND OVERVIEW

*T*he Digital Inking Student Superpower emphasizes using the power of the written word and digital tools to create conversation. Writing with digital ink empowers students to write in ways that are sharable and interactive. Importantly, writing in digital ink allows students to garner diverse feedback on their ideas, instantly accelerating progress. As students increase the strength of this superpower, the quality of their ability to catch and respond to the attention of an authentic audience will improve. Be sure to watch this transformation closely throughout the implementation of the instructional journey!

Specifically, this instructional journey encourages students to communicate to the lenses of different community stakeholders. Communication with intention requires a deep awareness of audience. This journey culminates with a media campaign challenge that showcases students' abilities to harness the power of all forms of digital ink!

DIGITAL INKING JOURNEY AT A GLANCE

WHAT SHOULD WE TWEET?

Instructional Journey Goals	1. Analyze a specific audience. 2. Write concisely for a specific audience. 3. Use digital tools to amplify the impact of your message.

General Progression	→ Effective messages begin with a specific audience in mind.
	   → Identifying the interests of others can help us be better writers.
	      → Digital ink gives us the power to share our messages with the audiences we choose (and many more)!

Connecting the Standards	Common Core State Standards for Reading, Writing, and Speaking and Listening • W.4—FOCUS STANDARD • W.6—FOCUS STANDARD • RI.2 • SL.1 • SL.2 • SL.3 National Curriculum Standards for Social Studies • Culture • Individual Development and Identity Common Core State Standards of Math Practice • SMP 1
Learning Activities	Lesson 1: Who's My Audience? How Do I Know? Lesson 2: What Are the Interests of My Audience? Lesson 3: Writing in Digital Ink
Tech Upgrades	• TuxPaint—http://tuxpaint.org • SMORE—www.smore.com • Twitter—www.twitter.com • Edmodo—www.edmodo.com
Final Assessment	Creating an Interactive Campaign

INSTRUCTIONAL JOURNEY GOALS

1. Analyze a specific audience.
2. Write concisely for a specific audience.
3. Use digital tools to amplify the impact of your message.

STUDENT-FRIENDLY
AUTHENTIC LEARNING PROBLEM

Words have power. How can we use "digital ink" to create interactive ideas that others will enjoy? Over the next few weeks, your job will be to use digital ink to spread your own ideas and the ideas of an important cause. So, how will you spread your message far and wide?

GENERAL PROGRESSION

→ Effective messages begin with a specific audience in mind.

    → Identifying the interests of others can help us be better writers.

        → Digital ink gives us the power to share our messages with the audiences we choose (and many more)!

CONNECTING THE STANDARDS

As this instructional journey and superpower are closely linked to critical literacy, the two focus standards come from the ELA Common Core. Areas that show increasing complexity are underlined for your reference (see the following table).

CONNECTIONS TO OTHER STANDARDS

COMMON CORE STATE STANDARDS FOR READING, WRITING, AND SPEAKING AND LISTENING

- **RI.2**—Determine central ideas or themes of a text and analyze their development; summarize the key supporting details and ideas.

- **SL.1**—Prepare for and participate effectively in a range of conversations and collaborations with diverse partners, building on others' ideas and expressing their own clearly and persuasively.

- **SL.2**—Integrate and evaluate information presented in diverse media and formats, including visually, quantitatively, and orally.

- **SL.3**—Evaluate a speaker's point of view, reasoning, and use of evidence and rhetoric.

NATIONAL CURRICULUM STANDARDS FOR SOCIAL STUDIES

- Culture
- Individual Development and Identity

COMMON CORE STATE STANDARDS OF MATH PRACTICE

- **SMP 1**—Make sense of problems and persevere in solving them.

CONNECTING THE STANDARDS

OVERALL STANDARD	GRADE 3	GRADE 4	GRADE 5
W.4: Produce clear and coherent writing in which the development, organization, and style are appropriate to task, purpose, and audience.	**W.4.3:** With guidance and support from adults, produce writing in which the development and organization are appropriate to task and purpose.	**W.4.4:** With guidance and support from adults, produce writing in which the development and organization are appropriate to task and purpose.	**W.4.5:** With guidance and support from adults, produce writing in which the development and organization are appropriate to task and purpose.
W.6: Use technology, including the Internet, to produce and publish writing and to interact and collaborate with others.	**W.6.3:** With guidance and support from adults, use technology to produce and publish writing (using keyboarding skills) as well as to interact and collaborate with others.	**W.6.4:** With some guidance and support from adults, use technology, including the Internet, to produce and publish writing as well as to interact and collaborate with others; demonstrate sufficient command of keyboarding skills to type a minimum of one page in a single sitting.	**W.6.5:** With some guidance and support from adults, use technology, including the Internet, to produce and publish writing as well as to interact and collaborate with others; demonstrate sufficient command of keyboarding skills to type a minimum of two pages in a single sitting.

LEARNING ACTIVITIES AND TECH UPGRADES

There are three lessons associated with this journey. In this book, lessons are defined as related series of student-driven explorations, not merely what will fit in a single class period. Actually, it is likely that each of these lessons will take several class periods to complete. After students explore all three lessons, provide them with the transfer task that follows to obtain summative data relative to the journey goals. All lesson resources (labeled for easy use) can be found on this Pinterest board:

http://pinterest.com/ssuperpowers/digital-inking-journey

(You can follow all Student Superpower Pinterest boards at **http://pinterest.com/ssuperpowers/boards**.)

LESSON 1: WHO'S MY AUDIENCE? HOW DO I KNOW?

For this lesson, students look at several author interviews. In small groups, students determine and sketch the audience that each author is trying to reach. These visualizations initiate an emphasis on writing for a specific audience that continues throughout the instructional journey. This sets the stage for the digital inking required in Lessons 2 and 3.

GENERAL PROCEDURES

1. Share *Eight Days: A Story of Haiti* by Edwidge Danticat with students. As you read to students, ask questions to probe students' interest.

2. After you share the story, show students the kid interview with the author. (The interview is accessible on the Pinterest page for this unit.)

3. Have students arrange themselves into pairs or groups of three. Provide each dyad or triad with a large piece of paper.

4. Given everything that students have learned about both the story and the author, tell students that they are going to play a "mind movie" game. Tell students to visualize the people for whom Edwidge Danticat wrote this story.

5. Students spend 10 minutes with their classmates drawing/sketching the people they have visualized.

6. Each group shares their image with the class and describes it. If needed, you may wish to provide students with a sentence starter such as, "I predict Edwidge Danticat wrote this story for _____ because _____."

7. As students share, write "big ideas" up on the whiteboard, chalkboard, or Smartboard. These could include things like:

   - "Her family" (Because Edwidge has family that was hurt or lost in the earthquake in Haiti.)

   - "Her children" (Because Edwidge wants her children to understand where she used to live.)

   - "Other kids in the United States" (Because Edwidge wants other kids to understand how she lived.)

8. Tell students to choose one of their favorite books from the classroom library. (You may also wish to take students to the actual library for this step.)

9. Once students select one of their favorite books, which may be at or below their reading level, they should use a piece of paper to draw all the people for whom they believe the author wrote the story.

10. Students should break into pairs and do the following:

    - Briefly describe the story to your partner.
    - Share the image of the people for whom the story was likely written and explain it.
    - Answer any questions from your partner.

    SWITCH ROLES!

11. As students share with their partners, they should come up to the board and put a star or check next to any theme that came up in their conversation. (They may need to add new themes as well. Guide them in this process as little as necessary.) This will help determine which themes/reasons/audiences are most popular for all authors. See Figure 6.1 for an example.

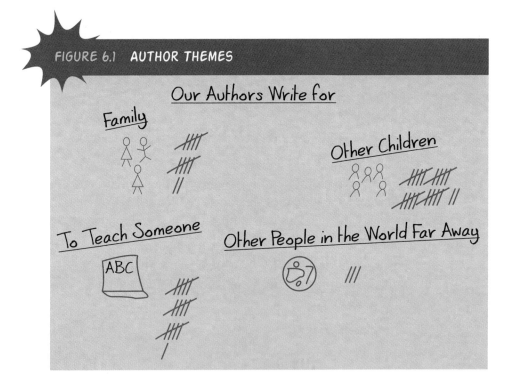

FIGURE 6.1   AUTHOR THEMES

If students finish early, encourage them to read their favorite books to each other!

12. When students finish Steps 8–11, bring them back to a place where they can easily view all the "big ideas." From here, hold a whole-group discussion. If possible, have a student lead the discussion. Consider the following questions:

    - What audiences are most common for our favorite authors?
    - Why is knowing who you are writing for so important?

- Do you think more people would read these books if they were on the Internet or posted in another place? Why or why not?

13. Students write an exit ticket that answers the following question:

- Who do authors write for? How do you know?

TECH UPGRADE FOR THIS LESSON

Try having students sketch their audience visualizations using TuxPaint.org, a free drawing program that includes stamps, lines, and many fun fonts. A direct link to this resource is available on the Pinterest board for this journey. Students can download, post, and share their work more easily when it is created with digital ink!

ARE THEY GETTING IT? POTENTIAL MISCONCEPTIONS AND SNAGS

In this lesson, some students may struggle to infer the people for whom an author might write a text or story. In this case, you may want to give students various options. This can help scaffold their thinking and avoid the development of stereotypes or misconceptions.

LESSON 2: WHAT ARE THE INTERESTS OF MY AUDIENCE?

Now that the class has a general idea about the most popular audiences for famous children authors, they are going to consider the interests of other audiences. Then, they will rewrite an article about coral reefs to appeal to a specific person or persons. The quality of their rewriting will depend on their ability to infer about the needs of others!

GENERAL PROCEDURES

1. Show the chart of "big ideas" from the previous day's lesson. One student leads a summary of the previous day's learning. He or she summarizes the learning and then calls on other students to add details. The student leader determines when the summary is sufficient.

2. Distribute paper to students with a specific person from one of the "big ideas" printed onto it. See Figure 6.2 for an example. Tell students that it is very important to truly understand your audience if you are a writer. You must understand and consider everything that your audience is thinking.

3. Ask students to close their eyes and imagine what it would be like to be the person on their card. Then, have students actively role-play how their person would perform the following actions:

- Go shopping
- Choose a movie to watch
- Play sports
- Sing a song

FIGURE 6.2   AUTHOR CARD

Note: This should be fun and maybe even a little silly. Students should "try on" their new personas and use words and voices and any other techniques they like.

4. After students have finished role playing, share a brief nonfiction passage about a Coral Reef with students. A direct link to this text is available on the Pinterest board for this journey. Students may read this on their own, in pairs, or with adult assistance. This passage is written at a Lexile level of 930L. You can substitute any nonfiction passage relevant to you and your students in this lesson. You may even wish to share different articles with different students. In short, it's the fit of the article for your class or group of students that matters most!

5. Students should use the article to create a list of facts about coral reefs. Then students should order the list according to the interests of the person on their card.

6. Students rewrite the nonfiction passage in its entirety *specifically* for the person on their card. Although they *cannot* change the facts in the article, they can change the order, the adjectives, and any opinions in the article. The information should be presented in a way that the person on their card really enjoys and understands the article. Students should be provided with approximately 30 minutes for the task. Imagine this as an extended journal prompt instead of a multiday writing assignment. The purpose of this activity is to help students practice for future instructional journey events and evaluations.

7. Set up stations around the room for students to engage in a gallery walk of the rewritten nonfiction articles. Each station should have a student's article and his or her card with the audience on it. Students should provide feedback to each other based on the following question:

   - Did this rewrite meet the needs of the person described on the card? How do you know?

SUPER TIP

GIVING STUDENTS OPPORTUNITIES FOR GALLERY WALKS CAN HELP THEM LEARN FROM EACH OTHER AND RECEIVE AUTHENTIC FEEDBACK.

8. Advise students that gallery walks are very similar to blogging, a form of digital inking.

9. Students walk around the classroom and leave notes for each other that respond to the question in Step 7.

10. Students generate as many responses as possible to each other's work during the gallery walk. Refer to these notes as "comments" that will give students a frame of reference when they begin to engage in digital inking. It is important to emphasize that feedback must answer the questions provided in Step 7 so that the feedback remains concrete and constructive.

11. After the gallery walk, have a whole-group discussion about what students noticed. Have a student lead this discussion if possible.

12. Students self-evaluate their performance on the lesson using the three-finger strategy for the following task: Did your writing have specific details to meet the needs of your audience?

    - Students hold up three fingers if they felt they did a *great* job.
    - Students hold up two fingers if they felt they did an OK job.
    - Students hold up one finger if they are really confused and need more help on this task.

TECH UPGRADE FOR THIS LESSON

Try using SMORE.com to publish some of the student writing samples in a digital space. SMORE is a free, easy-to-use poster creator that students and teachers can use to create one-page websites. Others can leave comments on pages, increasing the audience and feedback available to students. A direct link to this resource is available on the Pinterest board for this journey.

As students try to generate empathy for the person on their card, they may have difficulty inferring likely characteristics. If this happens, put students in pairs or groups of three to discuss their persona *before* the role play. This can give students more clarity before making meaning of their persona.

LESSON 3: WRITING IN DIGITAL INK

At this point, students are beginning to see the way that writing for a particular audience can affect an author's choices. In this lesson, students will have the opportunity to write in digital ink for a specific audience for a specific cause. Twitter (either in true digital or analog form) will be used as a communication medium for learners to garner as much feedback as possible.

Important Note: The context used for this activity (saving the orangutans via the increased use of sustainable palm oil) can be changed to any cause in your local area or community. It can also respond to students' specific needs. This is an example that you are welcome to use, but you can hone the digital inking superpower in many different ways!

GENERAL PROCEDURES

1. The teacher asks students the following question:

   - When we write with digital ink (on a computer), how is it different from writing on paper?

2. A student leader passes a ball to other students as they share responses to the question. When the student leader feels the question has been answered sufficiently, he or she passes the ball back to the teacher.

3. The teacher reminds students that they are trying to become people who write very well for a specific audience about a specific topic.

4. The teacher shares information about the Philadelphia Zoo Unless Project. (You can learn more by accessing the Pinterest board for this instructional journey.) As a part of this project, teens and preteens across the country work together to help increase the use of sustainable palm oil. The quest for manufacturers to gain access to palm oil has resulted in many orangutan habitats being destroyed. Kids are trying to help manufacturers to choose sustainable palm oil for their products (i.e., shampoo, body wash) instead of regular palm oil. They are also trying to inform their peers and parents about the best choices to make to help the orangutans survive and thrive.

5. Students break into three teams. These teams are named for the audience that they are targeting:

- Manufacturers
- Parents
- Peers

6. The teacher tells students that they are going to create a Twitter feed for 2 weeks to target these specific audiences. They will research and create messages that will encourage each audience to make good choices regarding sustainable palm oil products. There should be at least 14 messages (one per day).

Note: Twitter is a microblogging service. Each tweet can be 140 characters long and it can include a link or a picture. Twitter is often used to share messages worth spreading to a large audience in a short period of time. It is one of the most powerful mediums at this time for students when using the superpower of digital ink. Recent research from the Pew Internet Report found that Twitter is outpacing Facebook as the most popular social network among preteens and teens, so it's likely that they are familiar with the medium.

7. Students work in their groups to brainstorm potential messages for their Twitter feed. They should decide on the following:

- What will their Twitter handle (aka account name) be? It should be catchy and memorable.
- What will their Twitter bio be? It should be short and memorable.
- What will the image background be? It should respond to the specific needs and interests of the audience that they are trying to reach.
- What should each tweet say? (Only one sentence per tweet is recommended.)
- Should the tweets include links or images?

8. To begin, students should draft their tweets on sentence strips or pieces of paper. See the examples in Figure 6.3. Before any of the accounts or tweets are created, students should do a gallery walk, carefully observing each other's tweets. Students should provide feedback to each other using the following question:

- Do the tweets meet the needs of the audience? How do you know?

9. After students receive feedback on their drafts, they should revise their work and carefully consider the needs of their audience. For example, adults may respond to tweets that show them which shampoos they can buy for reasonable prices that use sustainable palm oil. Conversely, teens may respond to candies or other products that use sustainable palm oil.

Using sustainable palm oil will make your company appealing to people who like to be "GREEN". #projectunless
(109 characters)

Did you know your shampoo could be killing orangutans like this one? PHOTOLINK #shopsustainablepalmoil
(103 characters)

10. Students should begin their accounts and program their tweets. Students should also promote their Twitter accounts via e-mail or other methods to try to acquire followers during this time.

Note: If you are uncomfortable making Twitter accounts for your class to use, you can do this activity using paper sentence strips that are posted in a prominent location in the school for all to see! While this isn't truly digital inking, it certainly increases the students' access to an authentic audience of their peers.

11. Student groups monitor and use their Twitter accounts over the 2-week period and manage it accordingly under the guidance of the teacher. Students may wish to journal their progress over the period so that they can easily track growth over time at the end of the project. See an example in Figure 6.4.

12. At the end of the 2-week period, students should reflect on their progress via a whole-class discussion. A student leader should ask students the following questions:

- What worked?
- What didn't?
- Which messages were most effective for which audiences?
- How is digital ink different than regular writing?

TECH UPGRADE FOR THIS LESSON

Instead of using Twitter or sentence strips for this lesson, create an Edmodo account for your class. Edmodo is like a private Facebook account. Students can share digital inking messages within a private environment. Parents and community members can be invited to the Edmodo if you wish to do so. You

FIGURE 6.4   TWITTER JOURNAL

My Twitter Journal

    Day 1 –

        # of Retweets – 3

        # of Mentions – 4

        My Reflections:

            This was a tweet with only text.

            Maybe my audience needed a photo or

            link to learn more.

    Day 2 –

        # of Retweets – 22

        # of Mentions – 17

        My Reflections:

            Today I included a cute photo in my

            tweet. My audience really enjoyed this!

have greater control with this tool. A direct link to this tool is available on the Pinterest board for this journey.

ARE THEY GETTING IT? POTENTIAL MISCONCEPTIONS AND SNAGS

When it comes to digital inking, audience is really important. Students may not understand that gaining followers for their Twitter account is necessary to increasing both their audience and the impact of their message. You may need to help students acquire followers by putting updates in school or classroom newsletters or on a school Facebook page. Ensure that students understand the relationship between followers and readership. Get the word out to generate both excitement and feedback for the project!

FORMATIVE ASSESSMENT AND TRACKING STUDENT PROGRESS TOWARD GOALS

At the end of each lesson, students should self-assess their progress using the arrow continuum related to each journey goal using a yellow crayon. (See the following Formative Tracking Sheet for the arrow continuum.) You may also wish to have students provide notes or evidence justifying their rating. After students self-evaluate, you should assess their progress using a blue crayon. In every case where your rating agrees with the student's rating, it will create a "green light." This helps students to norm their ability to track their own progress. After using this strategy for some time, you'll likely find that most students are more stringent on their performance than you are!

Not only does this twofold method give you helpful information for future lessons, but it is also a strategy that significantly accelerates student achievement (Hattie, 2009). Go to the Pinterest page for this instructional journey to download the tracking sheet.

FINAL ASSESSMENT: HAVE YOUR GOALS BEEN ACHIEVED?

CREATING AN INTERACTIVE CAMPAIGN

For the final assessment of this unit, all three goals are measured using a single authentic task. In short, students will create an interactive campaign using digital media.

STUDENT-FRIENDLY PROMPT

Coca-Cola has been using polar bears to encourage people to drink their soda for decades. You can see an example of a commercial via the Pinterest page for this instructional journey. Coca-Cola chose polar bears because they thought that many different audiences would find them enjoyable and amusing.

However, Coca-Cola has developed a new soda that does not have any sugar and is much healthier than regular Coke. Due to this, Coca-Cola has decided that it's time to retire the polar bears and come up with a new, interactive, digital marketing campaign. You are the head of advertising at Coca-Cola and it's your job to create this new campaign.

In the campaign, you want to tell kids and parents that the new soda is better for you and also delicious.

FORMATIVE TRACKING SHEET: WHAT SHOULD WE TWEET?

Formative Tracking Sheet: What Should We Tweet?

Written messages are more impactful when shared. How can we use "digital ink" to create interactive ideas that others enjoy? Over the next few weeks, your job will be to use digital ink to spread your own ideas and the ideas of an important cause. So, how will you spread your message far and wide?

Unit Goals:

GOAL 1:	GOAL 2:	GOAL 3:
Analyze a specific audience.	Write concisely for a specific audience.	Use digital tools to amplify the impact of your message.

Learning Target for Goal 1: I can determine what my audience wants.

Lesson 1:
Exit Ticket: What do authors write for? How do you know?

Lesson 2:
Gallery Walk Feedback: Was I able to meet the needs of my audience with my writing? Were my peers?

Lesson 3:
Twitter Activity: Was I able to create a Twitter username and background that attracted the right followers?

Rate your own mastery of this learning target after each lesson. Remember that your rating can change over time:

New to Me ◄─────────────────────────────► I Got This!

Learning Target for Goal 2: I can write effectively for someone specific.

Lesson 2:
Lesson Task: What was the quality of your rewrite?

Lesson 3:
Lesson Task: What was the quality of your tweets?

Rate your own mastery of this learning target. Remember that your rating can change over time:

New to Me ◄─────────────────────────────► I Got This!

Learning Target for Goal 3: I can use a digital tool like Twitter so more people read what I write.

Lesson 3:
Lesson Task: What were the responses to my reflection questions after the 2-week Twitter project?

Rate your own mastery of this learning target. Remember that your rating can change over time:

New to Me ◄─────────────────────────────► I Got This!

SOURCE: This tool was inspired by a tool shared by Bill Ferriter in a blog post here:
http://blog.williamferriter.com/2013/02/16/my-middle-schoolers-actually-love-our-unit-overview-sheets

You may want to keep the following things in mind as you work on your campaign:

- You should make sure that all the messages you write are enticing to both children and their parents.

- You may want to choose a new mascot that both parents and kids will love.

- You may want to choose images or words that help people to understand that the new Coke is healthier.

- You may want to use digital ink to help your messages reach more people. This could include Facebook, Twitter, or Instagram.

- The quality of your campaign will be judged by parents and kids at your school.

STUDENT-FRIENDLY RUBRIC

RUBRIC INDICATOR	SUPERHERO	SIDEKICK	APPRENTICE
Knowing Your Audience	You know your audience and create content that they will understand/enjoy.	You know your audience, but you have some trouble coming up with content that they would like.	You are only beginning to learn about your audience.
Write Concisely and Clearly	You are able to write clearly and concisely using both a pen and digital ink.	You are able to write clearly and concisely almost all the time.	You write clearly or concisely sometimes. You often need lots of sentences to make your point.
Use Digital Tools to Amplify a Message	You are able to use several different digital tools effectively to amplify your message.	You are able to use one digital tool to increase the audience for your message.	You need to learn more before you feel comfortable using digital tools.

DIFFERENTIATION: MEETING THE NEEDS OF ALL LEARNERS

If you're still reading, it's likely that your classroom is a bustling, dynamic, diverse place. It's likely that you routinely make changes to your instruction to ensure that all students meet rigorous academic goals and hone their superpowers. Here are a few strategies you can use with this journey to make it more accessible for *all* of your students:

Provide greater specificity in the descriptions of the audience for each task. Some students may struggle to make inferences about a given audience if the description is brief.

Permit students to use speech to text applications when writing if needed. There are several free speech to text apps for mobile devices, such as Dragon Dictation, that can help students who struggle to record their thoughts. These tools should be permitted as supports.

Alter the writing of tweets from a creation task to a selection task. Provide students with a series of potential tweets that they can choose from a menu. You can use examples and nonexamples to make it more challenging. This could be used as a replacement or supplement to some aspects of the third lesson.

WINDOW INTO THE CLASSROOM

Max is a fifth-grade teacher in a suburban district. He has 26 learners in his class, and each learner is at a slightly different place. Although some of Max's students are very motivated, several students do not like writing activities. In fact, they openly groan when it is time for them to take out their journals. Due to this, Max wanted to help his students hone their Digital Inking Superpower.

Max started with Lesson 1. He wanted to try Tux Paint to have his students draw the intended audiences for their favorite chapter books, but the computer cart was signed out for the day. So, Max simply changed the activity to use regular paper. The students enjoyed the work, and many of them had never considered that an author writes a book *for a specific audience*. Max was really pleased when this takeaway surfaced on many of the exit slips after the lesson was finished.

As Max prepared to teach Lesson 2, he was concerned about text rigor. Max decided to alter the reading passage as he felt the Coral Reef passage provided in the journey was a bit too easy for his students.

Max's students responded *very* well to Lesson 2, and he was amazed at how well they were able to know their audience. The students were able to rewrite the nonfiction articles that Max provided with relevant details. However, Max felt that if he had given a few more details on the cards that described the audience, students may have been able to make more inferences. He plans to add more details for next time.

When Max planned to teach Lesson 3, he realized that his students were able to effectively write for a specific audience. His students even started initiating conversations about audience during reader's workshop without his prompts! He knew his students would be motivated by the use of Twitter because many of them had older brothers and sisters with accounts. He also thought that his students would be interested in working to save the orangutans because many of them were very interested in animals and endangered species.

When he introduced the task for Lesson 3, the students were very excited. They immediately began planning, and several groups continued to work during recess that day. Students garnered a large following for their Twitter accounts by advertising the effort in the school newsletter and at the local high school football game! In fact, students had so much fun that they remarked, "This is like writing FOR REAL!" Max noticed that much of the reticence in the class about writing had disappeared. In fact, his students continued writing on their Twitter feeds long after the project was formally finished.

For the final task, Max was interested to see if students would be able to translate their work with tweets to longer pieces of writing. The challenge was for students to create digital campaigns for Coca-Cola. Max was impressed with the time and care they put into testing out different messages and phrases for each audience. However, some groups needed support to make sure the messages for each group were unique and contained a complete message.

After the students completed the final task, Max displayed the student work in the foyer of his school. Parents and other community members left feedback for students about the effectiveness of their campaigns.

Max was glad he implemented the instructional journey, and he realized the power of digital inking for his students. Max's students were reenergized to write when an authentic audience was available. It certainly set a positive tone that carried through the rest of the year during writing time!

● ●

A QUESTION TO CONSIDER AS YOU REFLECT

- What audiences are available for your students' writing?

THE DESIGNING INSTRUCTIONAL JOURNEY

WHAT CAN YOU MAKE?

SUPERPOWER SUMMARY AND OVERVIEW

To excel in this world of endless change, students need to have the confidence and the skills to design and solve the challenges of their world. They need to understand how to identify what is missing and figure out a way to fix it. They must be creators, rather than simply consumers. By teaching students to engage with and change their worlds, teachers can create learning experiences that are relevant to their students' lives, training them to be people who change the world. Students are no longer simply the receptacles for information handed to them by all-knowing and wise teachers; they must become active participants in their learning and in their worlds.

There are specific steps that students can be taught to enable them to complete a design challenge and develop the Designing Superpower. In their book, *21st Century Skills*, Trilling and Fadel (2009, p. 97) identify the stages of design as Define, Plan, Do, and Review.

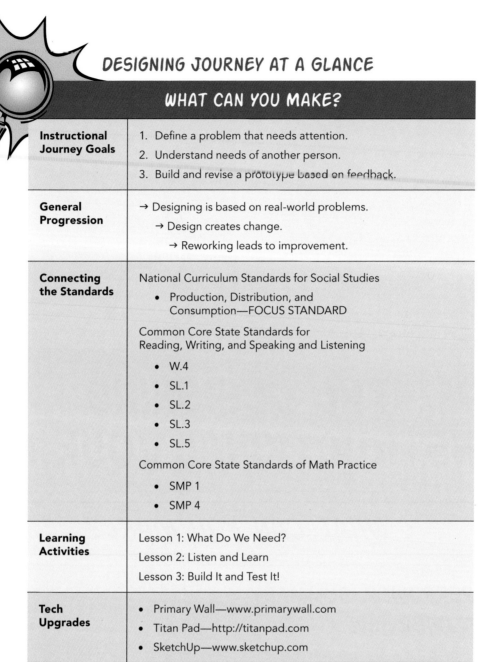

DESIGNING JOURNEY AT A GLANCE

WHAT CAN YOU MAKE?

Instructional Journey Goals	1. Define a problem that needs attention. 2. Understand needs of another person. 3. Build and revise a prototype based on feedback.
General Progression	→ Designing is based on real-world problems. 　→ Design creates change. 　　→ Reworking leads to improvement.
Connecting the Standards	National Curriculum Standards for Social Studies 　• Production, Distribution, and Consumption—FOCUS STANDARD Common Core State Standards for Reading, Writing, and Speaking and Listening 　• W.4 　• SL.1 　• SL.2 　• SL.3 　• SL.5 Common Core State Standards of Math Practice 　• SMP 1 　• SMP 4
Learning Activities	Lesson 1: What Do We Need? Lesson 2: Listen and Learn Lesson 3: Build It and Test It!
Tech Upgrades	• Primary Wall—www.primarywall.com • Titan Pad—http://titanpad.com • SketchUp—www.sketchup.com
Final Assessment	Design a School Bus

Stanford's d.school has a similar set of steps for design: Empathy, Define, Ideate, Prototype, Test. For both, it is an ongoing process, where new ideas are tested, reflected upon, and refined. The assumption is that there will be successes as well as failures along the way.

Many students have already started to develop their Designing Superpower, taking advantage of the possibilities available to them. They create "radio stations" on Pandora; they make movies and upload them to YouTube. They create their own shoes using tools provided by Nike and Vans to experiment with styles and colors that match their needs and desires at the time. Their world is not stagnant with others in control. They are ready to be change-makers! Becoming "Superheroes of Design" is a natural step for many of them.

In this journey, students use Stanford's d.school theory of design. They learn how to develop empathy, an understanding of the needs and desires of the person for whom they are designing. Students develop their initial plans based on what they learned, careful to incorporate the user's ideas into the scheme. They dream *big* dreams, reaching for new ways to meet the need. They build, in ways similar to Sylvia Martinez and Gary Stager's *Invent to Learn* (2013), using their hands as well as their minds to develop new ways of solving the problem. They experiment and test their solutions, making any necessary changes to improve it. Students develop their creativity and their resilience as they wrestle with real-world challenges.

INSTRUCTIONAL JOURNEY GOALS

1. Define a problem that needs attention.
2. Understand needs of another person.
3. Build and revise a prototype based on feedback.

STUDENT-FRIENDLY AUTHENTIC LEARNING PROBLEM

How can we solve the problems around us? We are always confronted with challenges that need solutions. Over the next few weeks, your job will be to create something new to bring about change that matters for those around you. Get ready to change the world!

GENERAL PROGRESSION

→ Designing is based on real-world problems.
   → Design creates change.
      → Reworking leads to improvement.

CONNECTING THE STANDARDS

As this instructional journey and superpower are closely linked to engineering design, the focus standard comes from the National Curriculum for Social Studies.

Consider this description from the National Council for Social Studies' (2010) website:

> **People have wants that often exceed the limited resources available to them.** The unequal distribution of resources necessitates systems of exchange, including trade, to improve the well-being of the economy, while the role of government in economic policy-making varies over time and from place to place. Increasingly, economic decisions are global in scope and require systematic study of an interdependent world economy and the role of technology in economic growth. As a result, a variety of ways have been invented to decide upon answers to four fundamental questions: What is to be produced? How is production to be organized? How are goods and services to be distributed and to whom? What is the most effective allocation of the factors of production (land, labor, capital, and entrepreneurship)?
>
> **In exploring this theme, students confront such questions as:** What factors influence decision-making on issues of the production, distribution, and consumption of goods? What are the best ways to deal with market failures? How does interdependence brought on by globalization impact local economies and social systems?

CONNECTIONS TO OTHER STANDARDS

COMMON CORE STATE STANDARDS FOR READING, WRITING, AND SPEAKING AND LISTENING

- **W.4**—Produce clear and coherent writing in which the development, organization, and style are appropriate to task, purpose, and audience.

- **SL.1**—Prepare for and participate effectively in a range of conversations and collaborations with diverse partners, building on others' ideas and expressing their own clearly and persuasively.

- **SL.2**—Integrate and evaluate information presented in diverse media and formats, including visually, quantitatively, and orally.

- **SL.3**—Evaluate a speaker's point of view, reasoning, and use of evidence and rhetoric.

- **SL.5**—Engage effectively in a range of collaborative discussions (one-on-one, in groups, and teacher-led) with diverse partners on topics and texts, building on others' ideas and expressing their own clearly.

COMMON CORE STATE STANDARDS OF MATH PRACTICE

- **SMP 1**—Make sense of problems and persevere in solving them.
- **SMP 4**—Model with mathematics.

LEARNING ACTIVITIES AND TECH UPGRADES

There are three lessons associated with this journey. In this book, lessons are defined as related series of student-driven explorations, not merely what will fit in a single class period. Actually, it is likely that each of these lessons will take several class periods to complete. After students explore all three lessons, provide them with the transfer task that follows to obtain summative data relative to the journey goals. All lesson resources (labeled for easy use) can be found on this Pinterest board:

http://pinterest.com/ssuperpowers/designing-journey

(You can follow all Student Superpower Pinterest boards at **http://pinterest.com/ssuperpowers/boards**.)

LESSON 1: WHAT DO WE NEED?

In this lesson, students are presented with a design challenge. In small groups, they work together to identify who the "users" are, the people for whom they will be designing. They develop interview questions to learn more about the needs of the user. They conduct "real-world" interviews to learn from actual people. They share what they discover and develop a set of goals for their design.

GENERAL PROCEDURES

1. Introduce the challenge. Explain to the students that the cafeteria is in need of new furniture and they have been asked to come up with designs to be considered. If possible, have someone in authority, the principal or head of the cafeteria, come to present the challenge to the students to give them a sense that there is an authentic audience.

2. Briefly describe the design process that they will be doing. Have the steps written on a poster or write them on the board. This is simply to give them an overview of what they will be doing, setting the stage. It is not necessary to go into detail.

   - Discover
   - Develop
   - Build
   - Test
   - Repeat

3. Take a walk to the cafeteria. They should take paper to write notes and make sketches. Encourage them to wander around the space and to especially look at the spaces that don't get much use.

4. Introduce the Right Questions strategy from www.rightquestion.org to develop a long list of questions to ask people they will interview. Arrange the chairs in a circle. Hand out a beanbag to a student. Explain that when one student is done sharing a question, he or she tosses the beanbag to the person sitting next to them. That student shares a question and tosses it on. A student can say "Pass" if he or she does not have a question. The teacher records all of the questions, hopefully projecting them onto a Smartboard or writes them on the board.

   - Ask as many questions as you can.
   - Do not stop to discuss, judge, or answer any questions.
   - Write down every question exactly as it is stated.
   - Change any statement into a question.

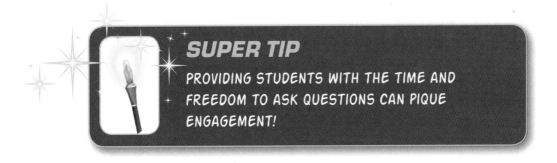

SUPER TIP

PROVIDING STUDENTS WITH THE TIME AND FREEDOM TO ASK QUESTIONS CAN PIQUE ENGAGEMENT!

5. Pose the following question for the students: When interviewing someone about the cafeteria, what should we ask? Hand the beanbag to a student. Record ideas on the board.

6. Have the students reread all of the questions and choose his or her top five questions. Have them put check marks next to their favorites to identify the class' top questions.

7. Organize the class into groups of four students. Explain that students will interview in pairs, with one asking the question and one recording the answer.

8. Have the groups each decide which questions they want to ask.

9. Each student creates an interview sheet.

TECH UPGRADE FOR THIS LESSON

Students could use Google Docs or other collaborative tools, such as Primary Wall, which allows students to create sticky notes and add them to a "wall"

UNLEASHING STUDENT SUPERPOWERS

that the teacher has created. If students are slow at typing, this would not be a good tool to use. It is important to not have the technology slow down the process of generating questions. A direct link to this resource is available on the Pinterest board for this journey.

ARE THEY GETTING IT? POTENTIAL MISCONCEPTIONS AND SNAGS

Some students can find the process of generating questions intimidating. Remind them that there is no judgment being made about the questions. The goal is to get as many different ideas up of the board for consideration. A crazy-sounding question may lead to new ways of thinking. Also, fully explain that saying "Pass" is a completely acceptable response. There might be another area of the school that works better for the students to create: the library, playground.

LESSON 2: LISTEN AND LEARN

In this lesson, the students develop a list of people who use the cafeteria. Each group is given a specific type of user: kindergartener, third grader, librarian, maintenance person, teacher. The group identifies one person who fits within their category of user and contacts that person to arrange for a time to conduct the interview and to later share their design. This is an important part of developing the Designing Superpower, because it creates the real-world context for the work of the student. To become an effective designer, it is necessary to understand who is going to be using the product that is being created. The students use the list of questions that was developed and interview their user. They then create the statement of design for what they will build. This lesson will take more than one class period as the students need to arrange for and conduct their interview. Here is how Stanford explains this step:

> A point-of-view (POV) is your reframing of a design challenge into an actionable problem statement that will launch you into generative ideation. A POV Analogy can be a concise and compelling way to capture how you define the design challenge (your POV!). A good analogy will yield a strong directive of how you go about designing the final solution. (d.school bootcamp bootleg, n.d., p. 22)

GENERAL PROCEDURES

1. Each student writes a list of people who use the cafeteria.

2. Students sit in a circle and share the people they identified. Record the people on the board. Again, students may say "Pass."

3. Put the students in groups of four and assign one user to each group.

4. Students meet in small groups to identify a specific person to interview that fits the user profile.

5. Students send the person they have identified a brief message to arrange two meeting times. The first meeting time is for the interview, and the second meeting time is to share the finalized design. See the Pinterest board for this journey to download a sample e-mail.

6. As arranged, students conduct the interview. Students take turns asking the questions and recording the answers.

7. Students work together, considering what they learned in the interview and thinking about what their user needs from their design. Create a Statement of Design. Fill in the blanks:

_____ has certain _____ that we can meet by
      [User]   [Needs or Desires]

_____.
    [Insight, New Ideas]

8. Students write their statement on poster-size paper to remind them of the purpose of their work. Each group's statement will differ, based on the needs of their user.

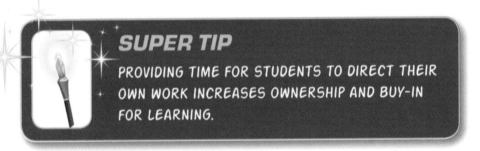

SUPER TIP

PROVIDING TIME FOR STUDENTS TO DIRECT THEIR OWN WORK INCREASES OWNERSHIP AND BUY-IN FOR LEARNING.

TECH UPGRADE FOR THIS LESSON

A collaborative tool, such as Titan Pad, could be used to create a Statement of Design. A direct link to this resource is available on the Pinterest board for this journey.

ARE THEY GETTING IT? POTENTIAL MISCONCEPTIONS AND SNAGS

Students may find it challenging to contact the person they need to interview. The teacher may want to make the necessary contacts with a variety of users before the challenge starts, identifying people who would be willing to take the time for the interview and the testing. Some students can find the interviewing process itself intimidating. Have them practice saying their questions for each other before they do the interview itself.

LESSON 3: BUILD IT AND TEST IT!

This lesson provides students with a chance to use their hands and build. "Making things and then making those things better is at the core of humanity" (Martinez & Stager, 2013). Students love to make their ideas come to life. For this lesson, students need access to cardboard and other supplies. Have students check recycling bins in advance and bring in unneeded "stuff" from home. Create a supplies area in the classroom. It is important, however, that the goal is not a perfect product, but a prototype that can be adjusted. The saying from Stanford's d.school, "Fail fast," is an important one. Designing is a process that takes lots of adjustment. The goal of this creation is to be a starting point. It will then be assessed and changed to better meet the needs of the user. The students may make one item as a group or make multiple items to meet the needs of the user.

GENERAL PROCEDURES

1. Watch "Caine's Arcade." This video is available on the Pinterest board for this journey.

2. Define the word *prototype*. One example from *Learner's Dictionary* is, "an original or first model of something from which other forms are copied or developed." Ask students how a prototype is different from a finished product.

3. Use the Marker Mic strategy and facilitate a whole-group discussion. Hand out the Marker Mic to one member of the group. Whoever has the Marker Mic can speak. Give each group a large sheet of paper to record their thinking.

   • Why was Caine successful?

   • How can we be successful in our building and creating time?

   • What will good group work look like?

   • What will good creation time look like?

4. Record student responses on the board. Develop a list of class guidelines.

5. Students return to the groups from Lesson 1, their design groups. Write the following questions on the board. Have each design group discuss them. Each group then creates an annotated sketch of the new cafeteria furniture.

   • What do we want to make?

   • Does it answer the needs of our user?

6. Set a time frame for the work to be done. Each group will then develop a Work Timeline that answers these questions.

   • What shall we make?

   • How shall we make it?

   • Who should do what part of the work?

7. Creation Time! This needs to be at least 60 minutes, but it could be much longer. It can be a bit chaotic, as the students are in charge. Play music during this time. While the students are working and building, the teacher is observing, offering reflection if asked. Do not volunteer ideas or suggestions. Use the "Yes, and . . ." to encourage students and challenge them to add to what they have done.

8. Allow time for cleanup.

9. Students share their prototype with the users that they interviewed. Students use feedback from the users to refine their design.

TECH UPGRADE FOR THIS LESSON

SketchUp could be used for planning before the creation stage. Working with their hands to bring their item to life is important, however, so make sure that the technology does not take the place of the building. A direct link to this resource is available on the Pinterest board for this journey.

ARE THEY GETTING IT? POTENTIAL MISCONCEPTIONS AND SNAGS

Students often are initially tentative to build, worried that it won't be perfect or they won't get it "right." They are not sure how to do it so it will look the way that they imagine it. It is important to remind them that they are creating something that will communicate their idea without perfection. If the students are extremely tentative about the creation process, they can build an arcade after watching "Caine's Arcade" as a warm-up activity.

FORMATIVE ASSESSMENT AND TRACKING STUDENT PROGRESS TOWARD GOALS

At the end of each lesson, students should self-assess their progress using the arrow continuum related to each instructional journey goal using a yellow crayon. (See the following Formative Tracking Sheet for the arrow continuum.) You may also wish to have students provide notes or evidence justifying their rating. After students self-evaluate themselves, you should assess their progress using a blue crayon. In every case where your rating agrees with the student's rating, it will create a "green light." This helps students to norm their ability to track their own progress. After using this strategy for some time, you'll likely find that most students are more stringent on their performance than you are! Not only does this twofold method give you helpful information for future lessons, but it is also a strategy that significantly accelerates student achievement (Hattie, 2009). Go to the Pinterest page for this instructional journey to download the tracking sheet.

FORMATIVE TRACKING SHEET: WHAT CAN YOU MAKE?

Formative Tracking Sheet: What Can You Make?

How do you design? What does it take to bring about change in the world? How do you solve a problem and create something new? Over the next few weeks, your job will be to investigate, design, and build.

Unit Goals:

GOAL 1:
Define a problem that needs attention.

GOAL 2:
Understand the needs of another person.

GOAL 3:
Build and revise a prototype based on feedback.

Learning Target for Goal 1: I can ask questions and learn what needs to be changed.

Lesson 1:
Lesson Task: I asked lots of questions
Lesson Task: I identified important information that I want to learn in an interview.

Lesson 2:
Lesson Task: I listened attentively to the user.

Lesson 3:
Lesson Task: I asked questions of my partners and shared my ideas.

Rate your own mastery of this learning target after each lesson. Remember that your rating can change over time:

New to Me ←——————————————————————————→ I Got This!

Learning Target for Goal 2: I can design to meet the needs of the user.

Lesson 2:
Lesson Task: I understood what the user wanted from the design.

Lesson 3:
Lesson Task: I worked well with my partners.

Rate your own mastery of this learning target. Remember that your rating can change over time:

New to Me ←——————————————————————————→ I Got This!

Learning Target for Goal 3: I build and rework based on what I have learned.

Lesson 3:
Lesson Task: I identified and made changes to our product.
Lesson Task: I cleaned up after myself and helped my partners clean up.

Rate your own mastery of this learning target. Remember that your rating can change over time:

New to Me ←——————————————————————————→ I Got This!

SOURCE: This tool was inspired by a tool shared by Bill Ferriter in a blog post: http://blog.williamferriter.com/2013/02/16/my-middle-schoolers-actually-love-our-unit-overview-sheets

FINAL ASSESSMENT: HAVE YOUR GOALS BEEN ACHIEVED?

DESIGN A SCHOOL BUS

For the final assessment in this instructional journey, students create an innovative school bus for kindergarteners. They apply what they have learned to interview, empathize, design, and test their ideas. They collaborate in design groups to complete this task. To kick off the task, a school bus driver talks to the class about his or her job. Students should also take a ride on a school bus to build interest in this project.

STUDENT-FRIENDLY PROMPT

Your design challenge is to build a school bus prototype for kindergarteners. We are going to ride on a school bus and interview kindergarteners to learn about their needs. Also, a school bus driver will be talking to us.

After you have gathered all of the information, dream big! What kind of amazing school bus could you design for these kindergarteners?

We will build and test your designs to see which group best meets the needs of the students and adult that you interviewed!

STUDENT-FRIENDLY RUBRIC

RUBRIC INDICATOR	SUPERHERO	SIDEKICK	APPRENTICE
Define a Problem That Needs Attention	You listened attentively to the users and identified their wants and desires.	You listened well and worked on allowing other ideas than yours to be significant.	You shared your ideas with the user instead of just listening.
Design Meets the Needs/ Desires of the User	You clearly understood what your user wanted and made that your top priority.	You understood what your user wanted but had some ideas of your own that were important to you.	You paid more attention to your own ideas than those of the user.
Final Design Product	The product was excellently planned and well built.	The product had a good design.	The product didn't match the user's needs.

DIFFERENTIATION: MEETING THE NEEDS OF ALL LEARNERS

This journey can easily be expanded to include a wide range of learners. To increase literacy, there are many articles on design thinking and effective designers. YouTube also has numerous videos about designing and bringing new ideas to life. The students could examine websites for examples of new styles of furniture before developing their own ideas. Below are a few specific examples of ways to differentiate this instructional journey:

- Identify one single user for the entire class or one type of furniture to help focus the students' attention.

- Provide more time for the students to build an arcade after watching "Caine's Arcade." Give time for them to play each other's games and assess what was successful about each. This provides an opportunity to build whatever they want, without the constraints of the needs and desires of the user. It also gives the students more of a chance to think about the process of creating something that effectively accomplishes its task.

- For the stronger students, challenge them to read articles and watch videos to develop their own step-by-step process for creating a successful design. Have them make posters for the classroom.

WINDOW INTO THE CLASSROOM

Liz is a third-grade teacher in a rural school. She has 22 students in her class, many of whom are struggling in school. Liz wanted to try a design challenge with her class as a way of showing that their work was significant. She also wanted to build a sense of community among her students and saw these lessons as a way to do that. She liked the idea of using the cafeteria as the focus, because her school was definitely in need of some improvements in the look and feel of their cafeteria.

Liz decided to ask her principal to come in to introduce the project. She wanted the students to know from the start that someone outside of their room would be paying attention to their work. Ms. Temple smiled and explained that their teacher had been telling her about the class and their positive energy, and she wanted to recruit them to design new furniture for the cafeteria. The students couldn't believe their ears. Their hands went flying into the air, as soon as she finished.

"Will you really look at them?"

"Yes, indeed I will!"

"Will we really make them? For real?"

Liz spoke up. "We will design them and share them with Ms. Temple."

"Will they really end up in the cafeteria?"

"Let me see your designs, and then perhaps we will be able to find some money to have them made. No promises, but I can't wait to see what you come up with," Ms. Temple answered.

The students were totally hooked. They had a real challenge with a real audience for their work.

Liz explained briefly that they would be following a design process. She put them into groups of three and told them that they were going to go on an investigation walk. She asked them to take a piece of paper and a pencil with them. She led them to the cafeteria and gave them 10 minutes to observe and record. The homework for that night was to bring in items that could be used for the building part of the work: recyclables, unused craft supplies, etc.

Back in the classroom, the students easily identified who used the cafeteria and generated an extensive list of questions, using the Right Question strategy. They loved the rules for asking questions, finding it liberating to simply say whatever came into their heads about the topic. While a few students used the "Pass," for the most part, students had lots of questions they wanted to share.

The biggest challenge came in coordinating the interviews. She had seven different users: three students of different ages and four adults, which made it very complicated to find times that worked for every group. Next year, Liz plans on doing that part of the work herself, setting up times with the different users ahead of time. She also is considering having fewer users, perhaps with two groups working with a single user.

Liz's biggest surprise came during the building stage of the project. The classroom was filled with noises and scraps of material, and the students were totally engaged. She wandered around, giving positive comments but working hard to avoid any form of critique. She let them do the work that they wanted to do. The students themselves gave each other feedback, both to other members of their own group and to other groups. They loved the energy that came from actually making their ideas three-dimensional.

After having students share their work with the original user, Liz was amazed at how quickly they set about reworking their original designs. They wanted to improve. There was none of the normal discouragement that usually happened after their work was evaluated. It mattered to them that they created something of value that actually met the needs and desires of their user, so the extra work was worth it. Liz realized that the process had indeed created a community of designers in her classroom, ones who were ready and eager to tackle their next challenge.

● ●

A QUESTION TO CONSIDER AS YOU REFLECT

- What ways are there for students to design and build in the classroom?

THE GAMING INSTRUCTIONAL JOURNEY

MAKE LIFE MORE FUN!

SUPERPOWER SUMMARY AND OVERVIEW

For most of our students, gaming is a part of everyday life. "Teens, Videogaming, and Civics," a report published by the Pew Internet & American Life Project, states that 97% of American youth between the ages of 12 to 17 play electronic games regularly (Lenhart, 2008).

Kids love video games because well-constructed games increase motivation and engagement. Game designers can capture time, attention, and resources by putting people into a state of "flow." Ralph Koster, a well-known game designer, writes,

"With games, learning is the drug" (Koster, 2005).

As students increase the strength of this superpower, their ability to motivate and engage others will increase. They will create settings and situations where people want to try new things, do new work, and gain an epic win!

Specifically, this instructional journey encourages students to gamify real life situations.

Kevin Werbach and Dan Hunter, authors of *For the Win*, state,

"There's nothing derogatory in the observation that education and work are really just games. We began to ask ourselves, why not make them better games?" (2012, p. 12).

This journey culminates with a gamification challenge to reimagine problems or challenges in students' schools and communities.

GAMING JOURNEY AT A GLANCE

MAKE LIFE MORE FUN!

Instructional Journey Goals	1. Design an enjoyable way to learn or work. 2. Create a set of rules/constraints that are aligned to a specific goal. 3. Increase motivation to do a task or learn something.

General Progression	→ Playing games is fun.
	    → Games can be analog or digital.
	        → Games can accomplish important work.

Connecting the Standards	Common Core State Standards for Reading, Writing, and Speaking and Listening • W.2—FOCUS STANDARD • W.4—FOCUS STANDARD • R.10 • W.5 • W.6 • SL.1 • SL.2 • SL.3 National Curriculum Standards for Social Studies • People, Places, and Environment • Power, Authority, and Governance Common Core State Standards of Math Practice • SMP 1
Learning Activities	Lesson 1: Hacking Monopoly Lesson 2: Gamification Hunt Lesson 3: Make Your Own Game
Tech Upgrades	• Photo Peach—http://photopeach.com • Gamestar Mechanic—http://gamestarmechanic.com • Build Your Wild Self—www.buildyourwildself.com
Final Assessment	Gamify Your Homework

1. Design an enjoyable way to learn or work.
2. Create a set of rules/constraints thatr are aligned to a specific goal.
3. Increase motivation to do a task or learn something.

STUDENT-FRIENDLY AUTHENTIC LEARNING PROBLEM

Do you play games? Games encourage us to use many different parts of our brains and bodies. Over the next few weeks, your job will be to turn ordinary activities into fun games for you and your classmates. Can you make every part of life as fun as your favorite game?

GENERAL PROGRESSION

→ Playing games is fun.
  → Games can be analog or digital.
    → Games can accomplish important work.

CONNECTING THE STANDARDS

As this instructional journey and superpower are closely linked to critical literacy, the two focus standards come from the ELA Common Core. Areas that show increasing complexity are underlined for your reference (see the following table).

CONNECTIONS TO OTHER STANDARDS

COMMON CORE STATE STANDARDS FOR
READING, WRITING, AND SPEAKING AND LISTENING

- **R.10**—Read and comprehend complex literary and informational texts independently and proficiently.

- **W.5**—Develop and strengthen writing as needed by planning, revising, editing, rewriting, or trying a new approach.

- **W.6**—Use technology, including the Internet, to produce and publish writing and to interact and collaborate with others.

CONNECTING THE STANDARDS

OVERALL STANDARD	GRADE 3	GRADE 4	GRADE 5
W 2: Write informative/ explanatory texts to examine and convey complex ideas and information clearly and accurately through the effective selection, organization, and analysis of content.	**W.2.3:** Write informative/ explanatory texts to examine a topic and convey ideas and information clearly. a. Introduce a topic and group related information together, include illustrations when useful to aiding comprehension. b. Develop the topic with facts, definitions, and details. c. Use linking words and phrases within categories of information. d. Provide a concluding statement or section.	**W.2.4:** Write informative/ explanatory texts to examine a topic and convey ideas and information clearly. a. Introduce a topic and group related information <u>in paragraphs and sections</u>, include illustrations when useful to aiding comprehension. b. Develop the topic with facts, definitions, concrete details, quotations, or other information and examples related to the topic. c. Link ideas within categories of information using words and phrases. d. Use precise language and domain-specific vocabulary to inform or explain about a topic. e. Provide a concluding statement or section related to the information or explanation presented.	**W.2.5:** Write informative/ explanatory texts to examine a topic and convey ideas and information clearly. a. Introduce a topic clearly, provide a general observation and focus, and group related information logically; include formatting, illustrations, and multimedia when useful to aiding comprehension. b. Develop the topic with facts, definitions, concrete details, quotations, or other information and examples related to the topic. c. Link ideas within categories of information using words, phrases, and <u>clauses</u>. d. Use precise language and domain-specific vocabulary to inform or explain about a topic. e. Provide a concluding statement or section related to the information or explanation presented.

OVERALL STANDARD	GRADE 3	GRADE 4	GRADE 5
W.4: Produce clear and coherent writing in which the development, organization, and style are appropriate to the task.	**W.4.3:** With guidance and support from adults, produce writing in which the development and organization are appropriate to task and purpose.	**W.4.4:** With guidance and support from adults, produce writing in which the development and organization are appropriate to task and purpose.	**W.4.5:** With guidance and support from adults, produce writing in which the development and organization are appropriate to task and purpose.

- **SL.1**—Prepare for and participate effectively in a range of conversations and collaborations with diverse partners, building on others' ideas and expressing their own clearly and persuasively.
- **SL.2**—Integrate and evaluate information presented in diverse media and formats, including visually, quantitatively, and orally.
- **SL.3**—Evaluate a speaker's point of view, reasoning, and use of evidence and rhetoric.

NATIONAL CURRICULUM STANDARDS FOR SOCIAL STUDIES

- People, Places, and Environments
- Power, Authority, and Governance

COMMON CORE STATE STANDARDS OF MATH PRACTICE

- **SMP 1**—Make sense of problems and persevere in solving them.

LEARNING ACTIVITIES AND TECH UPGRADES

There are three lessons associated with this journey. In this book, lessons are defined as related series of student-driven explorations, not merely what will fit in a single class period. Actually, it is likely that each of these lessons will take several class periods to complete. After students explore all four lessons, provide them with the transfer task that follows to obtain summative data relative to the journey goals. All lesson resources (labeled for easy use) can be found on this Pinterest board:

http://pinterest.com/ssuperpowers/gaming-journey

(You can follow all Student Superpower Pinterest boards at **http://pinterest.com/ssuperpowers/boards**.)

LESSON 1: HACK MONOPOLY

For this lesson, students hack the game of Monopoly. In small groups, students use the game pieces from Monopoly as well as any other classroom materials to create a new game. This process is collaborative, and it helps them to realize that a game can be both engaging and confusing. This sets the stage for the gaming challenges required in future lessons.

Note: The authors were first introduced to this activity by Meeno Rami and Chad Sansung at the Educon conference in Philadelphia. This lesson is adapted from that experience and several other hack jams they've attended. You can learn more about the National Writing Project hack jams here: http://nwphackjam.tumblr.com.

GENERAL PROCEDURES

1. Begin by giving students a game of Monopoly as well as any other classroom materials available. (You may wish to substitute another board game for Monopoly.) Rubber bands, Play-Doh, small plastic figurines, and sticky notes work great for this activity. Just putting these materials in view heightens intrigue and serves as a great hook for this journey!

2. Have a whole-group discussion on collaboration during group work. This is important so that students are considerate of each other as they distribute materials and create rules throughout the lesson.

3. Provide students with the following rules:

   - The person who has the most pets gets to go first.
   - The first person gives out the materials as he or she sees fit. (Be sure to tell students that this does not have to follow the traditional rules. They can make changes if they like.)
   - From there, each person takes a turn playing the game. Each person gets to make up a new rule at the beginning of his or her turn. (Groups may want to designate one person as the "recorder" to jot down each rule as it's created.)
   - Play continues for 20 minutes.

4. After time is up and students have cleaned up their game boards, present students with the following questions:

   - Was the game you created fun? Why or why not?
   - What makes games fun?
   - What makes games frustrating?

5. Students jot their answers to the questions in Step 4. Then have all students join a whole-group discussion to further explore the questions.

6. As students share their reflections, record commonalities on the board to provide students with a visual way to organize their thinking.

7. Remind students that they will be designing games as a part of this learning experience. Emphasize that good game design creates positive experiences.

8. Students write an exit ticket that answers the following question:

- What makes a game fun? How do you know?

TECH UPGRADE FOR THIS LESSON

Students will have a lot of fun and get very creative as they invent new rules for their game during Step 3 in the lesson above. You may wish to have students take photos of the various game boards and piece configurations throughout the game play. If students take pictures, they can put these pictures into a slideshow quickly and easily using Photo Peach. Photo Peach can be used for free at http://photopeach.com. Students will enjoy revisiting this learning activity again and again via a slideshow!

ARE THEY GETTING IT? POTENTIAL MISCONCEPTIONS AND SNAGS

In this lesson, some students may create rules that directly conflict with each other. Often, this will cause students to freeze up. If this happens, you should work with students to create a rule or series of rules that negates the conflicting set.

LESSON 2: GAMIFICATION HUNT

At this point in the journey, students have some ideas about what makes a good game. More specifically, students' exit tickets from Lesson 1 should also indicate that they understand what makes a game enjoyable, motivating, and fun. Now, students are going to explore everyday life situations.

The word "gamification" means that you take an ordinary situation or task and apply the principles of game design to increase engagement, motivation, and fun. Students will analyze a few examples of gamification in this lesson.

GENERAL PROCEDURES

1. Show students photos or describe game boards from the previous lesson. Have students retell the previous day's events by passing around one of the Monopoly tokens. Try to encourage students to take ownership of this activity, and refrain from entering the conversation unless it is necessary to dispel a misconception.

2. Show students a list of game mechanics and tell them that they are going to be "on the lookout" for these qualities as they explore a few different videos and readings.

- List of Game Mechanics

  o Challenges

  o Chance

  o Collecting things

  o Competition

- Cooperation/Working together
- Getting rewards or prizes
- Taking turns
- Winning

3. Have students describe what each word means and take notes on chart paper. This will support students who may not be familiar with all the words or concepts listed.

4. Once students are comfortable with the terms, tell them that they are going on a gamification hunt. Students will break into small teams and go on a gallery walk around the classroom. A gallery walk is a series of stations where students look at a specific piece of information and respond to it.

5. The media for each station of the gallery walk has been provided on the Pinterest board for this unit. Have a laptop or tablet with each site from the Pinterest board queued up for students in advance.

   - **Station 1: Duolingo.** This quick video shows students that they can learn a new language and translate the Internet by playing a free game.
   - **Station 2: Recycle Bank.** This quick video shows how people can get rewards and points when they recycle.
   - **Station 3: Piano Staircase.** This brief video shows how making something more fun can motivate people to do something that they might not do otherwise.
   - **Station 4: Tio for Turning Off Lights.** This article shows how a glow frog helps students turn off the lights and earn points for being "green" and saving electricity.

6. Students spend at least 5 minutes at each station. While there, they watch the video and read the website. Then, they record all the game mechanic elements they noticed on their Gallery Walk Sheet. You can download the Gallery Walk Sheet on the Pinterest board for this journey. Students are encouraged to talk to each other and discuss each video.

7. After students have visited every station, they then come together as a whole group and record their thinking as a class. A set of four bar graphs, one for each station, can be used to record these data. See Figure 8.1 for an example.

8. Students work as a class to analyze the bar graph for each station/video/article. Use the following guiding questions:

   - What made all of these stations alike?
   - What made them different?

- How did using things from our game mechanics list make the regular task (i.e., walking up the stairs, recycling) more fun?

9. As a final brainstorm, students think of experiences where they encounter some of these elements. This brainstorm can be verbal or written, depending on the needs of your students. Examples may include a frequent shopper grocery point system or a soccer game.

10. Students self-evaluate their performance on the lesson using the three-finger strategy for the following task: Did you find all the game mechanics in the examples?

- Students hold up three fingers if they felt they did a *great* job.
- Students hold up two fingers if they felt they did an OK job.
- Students hold up one finger if they are really confused and need more help on this task.

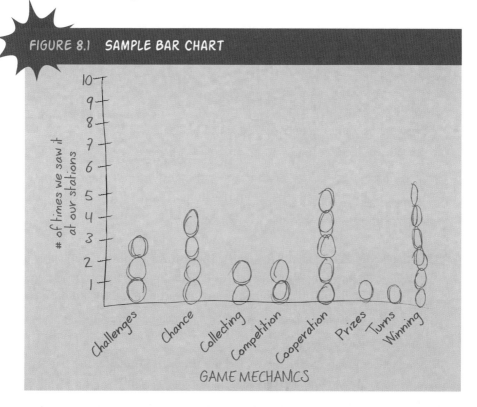

FIGURE 8.1   SAMPLE BAR CHART

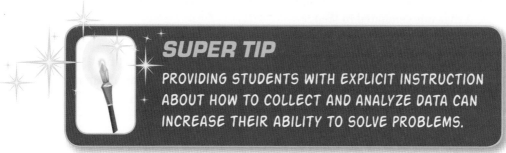

SUPER TIP

PROVIDING STUDENTS WITH EXPLICIT INSTRUCTION ABOUT HOW TO COLLECT AND ANALYZE DATA CAN INCREASE THEIR ABILITY TO SOLVE PROBLEMS.

If students are very interested in making a video game, they can check out Gamestar Mechanic. With a free account, students can play and design their first question that teaches them more intricate knowledge of game design in a digital format.

ARE THEY GETTING IT? POTENTIAL MISCONCEPTIONS AND SNAGS

Some students may struggle with the complexity of the list provided for the different game mechanics. You may shorten the list provided, only providing students with three to five different game mechanics.

LESSON 3: MAKE YOUR OWN GAME

During the third lesson in this journey, students should recognize game mechanics. They should also be comfortable exploring many ordinary tasks that are specially designed to be like games. In this lesson, students will have the opportunity to redesign a daily task using different game mechanics. This task will prepare students for the final assessment in this journey.

GENERAL PROCEDURES

1. The teacher asks students the following questions:

    - How do games help us?
    - Why are games fun to play?

2. A student leader passes a ball to other students as they share responses to the question. When the student leader feels the question has been answered sufficiently, he or she passes the ball back to the teacher.

3. The teacher asks students to silently brainstorm all of the things that they *do not* like to do in their daily life. This could include chores, soccer practice, nightly reading, or any other undesirable activity.

4. Once the silent brainstorm is finished, the teacher asks selected students to share their ideas aloud.

5. The teacher records the answers. Then students decide on the five to six topics that are most disliked.

6. Students break up into groups, and each group takes a task or topic that was generated in Step 5.

7. Students are provided with a prompt. "Make it FUN to do this task! You can add points, rewards, or competition. Reinvent how this task is completed so that everyone will be eager to participate. Refer to your list of game mechanics to help you. You can create any materials needed for your game using paper or other classroom materials."

SUPER TIP

PROVIDING STUDENTS WITH MANY OPPORTUNITIES TO COLLABORATE WITH THEIR PEERS INCREASES THEIR SUPERPOWERS.

8. Provide students with at least 1 hour to design and create materials for their games. As students work through the process, they should consider the following things:

   - Do I need any props or game pieces for my game?
   - Which elements of game mechanics do I want to use?
   - Are the rules clear and easy to understand?
   - How will I explain my game to people?
   - Does the game make people excited?

9. After students have designed their game, each group takes turns sharing their work with the class. If possible, the class can engage in gameplay.

10. After each presentation, the class should be able to ask questions for clarification. The class can use the "Two Stars and a Wish" protocol to provide feedback to their peers. The "Two Stars and a Wish" protocol requires someone to say two things they really liked about the design and one thing they wish would have been done differently. This helps to ensure that students receive ample warm and cool feedback.

11. After all presentations are finished, students independently reflect on their work. This can be written in a journal if desired.

12. Students write an exit ticket that answers the following questions: How did I do? Did my efforts make a boring task more fun and more exciting? How do I know?

TECH UPGRADE FOR THIS LESSON

It is likely that students will want interesting avatars to include with their games. Build Your Wild Self is a tool that can help with this. The tool allows students to create animated avatars that combine human and animal parts. You can use Build Your Wild Self free of charge at www.buildyourwildself.com. This site simply provides a small tech upgrade to motivate and embellish students' designs.

ARE THEY GETTING IT? POTENTIAL MISCONCEPTIONS AND SNAGS

Some students may fixate on one or two game mechanics, such as rewards or points. Children may need some prompting to expand their designs beyond these basic measures. If you notice that a team is ignoring options such as cooperation or collecting items, you may want to have a mini-conference with them to help them diversify their design. Another common problem is that students try to include all of the elements of game mechanics in their design. Again, hold a mini-conference with a group if you notice this and provide targeted feedback to help students revise their game.

FORMATIVE ASSESSMENT AND TRACKING STUDENT PROGRESS TOWARD GOALS

At the end of each lesson, students should self-assess their progress using the arrow continuum related to each journey goal using a yellow crayon. (See the following Formative Tracking Sheet for the arrow continuum.) You may also wish to have students provide notes or evidence justifying their rating. After students self-evaluate, you should assess their progress using a blue crayon. In every case where your rating agrees with the student's rating, it will create a "green light." This helps students to norm their ability to track their own progress. After using this strategy for some time, you'll likely find that most students are more stringent on their performance than you are!

Not only does this twofold method give you helpful information for future lessons, but it is also a strategy that significantly accelerates student achievement (Hattie, 2009). Go to the Pinterest board for this instructional journey to download the tracking sheet.

FINAL ASSESSMENT: HAVE YOUR GOALS BEEN ACHIEVED?

GAMIFY YOUR HOMEWORK

For the final assessment of this instructional journey, students will be tasked with an important problem. They will use game mechanics to make homework more fun! All three superpower goals will be measured through this single authentic task. To make the task more relevant, consider allowing some of the gamified homework designs to be used in class! Not only will this increase motivation for the task, but it will also increase motivation for future homework assignments. It's a win-win!

STUDENT-FRIENDLY PROMPT

Today, you're going to be gamifying something that many children don't find fun: homework. Think about it; making homework into a game could pump up the brains of you and your classmates!

This is no easy task. You'll need to carefully consider all the ways to make homework fun and exciting. To help you, refer to the list of game mechanics

FORMATIVE TRACKING SHEET: MAKE LIFE MORE FUN!

Formative Tracking Sheet: Make Life More Fun!
Do you play games? Games encourage us to use many different parts of our brains and bodies. Over the next few weeks, your job will be to turn ordinary activities into fun games for you and your classmates. Can you make every part of life as fun as your favorite game?

Unit Goals:

GOAL 1:	GOAL 2:	GOAL 3:
⌕ Create a set of rules/constraints that are aligned to a specific goal.	⌕ Increase motivation to do a task or learn something.	⌕ Design an enjoyable way to learn or work.

Learning Target for Goal 1: I can make new rules for a game that everyone enjoys.

Lesson 1:
Lesson Task: Hack Monopoly

Lesson 1:
Exit Ticket: What makes a game fun? How do you know?

Lesson 2:
Gallery Walk Feedback: Was I able to meet the needs of my audience with my writing? Were my peers?

Rate your own mastery of this learning target after each lesson. Remember that your rating can change over time:

New to Me ◄─────────────────────────────────► I Got This!

Learning Target for Goal 2: I know what motivates people to play a game.

Lesson 2:
Lesson Task: Chart of game mechanics created after the gallery walk

Lesson 2:
Exit Ticket: Student self-evaluation (three, two, one finger)

Rate your own mastery of this learning target. Remember that your rating can change over time:

New to Me ◄─────────────────────────────────► I Got This!

Learning Target for Goal 3: I can make something that people don't like to do fun and enjoyable using games.

Lesson 3:
Lesson Task: How did my classmates respond to the game I designed with my team? Was my game fun?

Rate your own mastery of this learning target. Remember that your rating can change over time:

New to Me ◄─────────────────────────────────► I Got This!

SOURCE: This tool was inspired by a tool shared by Bill Ferriter in a blog post: http://blog.williamferriter.com/2013/02/16/my-middle-schoolers-actually-love-our-unit-overview-sheets

you know. Remember to use *just the right amount* of game mechanics so that the game is fun and accomplishes the task at hand.

Create the rules for your game as well as any props you will need. Be prepared to present your design to a tough audience: your teacher and fellow students!

If your design is good enough, your teacher may use this game for *your* homework. So, what are you waiting for? Get started on this challenge right away!

STUDENT-FRIENDLY RUBRIC

RUBRIC INDICATOR	SUPERHERO	SIDEKICK	APPRENTICE
Clear Rules That Are Easy to Follow	Your rules are exciting and easy to follow.	Your rules are easy to follow.	Your rules are confusing.
Good Use of Game Mechanics	You use a variety of game mechanics so that your game is fun and exciting to play.	You use some game mechanics.	You aren't sure which game mechanics to use.
Overall Engaging Design	The design choices you selected for your game were perfectly tailored to fit the needs of your audience.	The design choices you selected were exciting and attractive.	You weren't sure which design choices to select.

DIFFERENTIATION: MEETING THE NEEDS OF ALL LEARNERS

This journey is extremely flexible, and it can be adjusted to meet the needs of your learners. For example, you may wish to increase literacy in this unit by sharing articles and written examples of game design with students. Students could even analyze sets of game directions! Conversely, you could greatly simplify this journey by reducing the number of game mechanics that you introduce to students or through additional modeling. In short, be sure to provide your students with exactly what they need to hone their Gaming Superpower! Below are a few specific suggestions to adjust this journey:

Show students many different examples of board games and provide them with an opportunity to identify what makes them similar. Some students may not be ready for the Hack Monopoly lesson without prior prompting. In this case, have students explore many different board games to notice their similarities. Refining students' concepts of games in general can better prepare them for the first lesson.

Increase the rigor of the gallery walk in Lesson 2 by including nonfiction text articles from the Web. The Internet has many articles about gamification and game design. To challenge students, print out some of these articles and provide them as alternate stations during the gallery walk. This can provide them with more details.

Increase the rigor of the final task by making the context less familiar. If your students are ready for a challenge, then give them the opportunity to gamify something less familiar than the homework process. For example, they could gamify the selection of healthy foods in the cafeteria.

WINDOW INTO THE CLASSROOM

Sherry is a fourth-grade teacher in a rural district. She had never heard of gamification before reading this journey, and she wasn't sure if her students needed to practice their Gaming Superpower. However, out of curiosity, she asked her students about video games one day. Every child in her class played video games at home! For some of her students, it was their favorite recreational activity. This piqued her curiosity, so she decided to try the journey.

Sherry started with Lesson 1. She was instantly amazed by her students' creativity when they began to "Hack Monopoly." Many of the rules they created made the game more fast paced and easy to play. Some of the students created new game pieces that would appeal to smaller children. After the lesson, students regularly began taking home her classroom games at night!

Sherry considered the needs of her class when planning Lesson 2. She quickly realized that her students would be able to handle rigorous reading passages in addition to the stations suggested in the journey. After a quick Google search, Sherry was able to locate three articles appropriate for her students. She added these stations to the rotation, allowing her to make the groups smaller and more individualized.

Sherry was eager to begin Lesson 3 where students brainstorm things they do not like to do. To her delight, many students identified chores at home and on the farm, which are perfect for gamification. Sherry's students worked diligently on the project, and a few students even got their siblings involved in "game testing!" Some students struggled to find the right amount of game mechanics, and Sherry needed to hold several mini-conferences with some teams.

Student motivation for the task skyrocketed when Sherry was able to have a game designer video chat with the class. He told the class that he was "impressed by their knowledge" and he told them that three game mechanics was usually the right amount. Students immediately took this advice to heart and revised their designs . . . *again*. Sherry noticed that students who usually tried to finish their work as quickly as possible were revising their work multiple times. In short, she was thrilled!

When students shared their designs with each other at the end of Lesson 3, many referenced the words of the game designer who virtually visited their class a few days earlier. Sherry was really impressed by their ability to use the feedback the game designer provided very flexibly!

For the final task, Sherry had her students redesign homework. However, Sherry received clearance from the principal that the entire school could play the new "homework game" for a week. All of the groups came up with good designs, and the principal agreed to try all the designs for a week. Students across the entire school were very excited to try out a new "homework game" each week!

Sherry felt very empowered by the journey, and she noticed that students started taking more ownership over their learning in lots of different areas. Sherry's students brought this energy to all of their subjects!

● ●

A QUESTION TO CONSIDER AS YOU REFLECT

- How can you put students in a state of "flow" more often by using games?

THE SUPERPOWER AUDIT

HOW AM I DOING?

WE SHOULD NOT JUDGE PEOPLE BY THEIR PEAK OF EXCELLENCE; BUT BY THE DISTANCE THEY HAVE TRAVELED FROM THE POINT WHERE THEY STARTED.

—HENRY WARD BEECHER (N.D.)

HOW CAN I TRACK PROGRESS?

Transforming your classroom takes focus and attention, but it's worth it. Classrooms where students own their learning tend to have fewer behavior problems and a more pleasant classroom climate (Lai, 2011). Further, Marzano's (2003) research reminds us that teachers are the number one factor affecting student achievement in the classroom. The goal is to shift your practice, putting kids in control of their learning. In short, your hard work will have a big impact on student learning and make your teaching experience more positive!

As the positive benefits of a student-driven classroom don't develop overnight, it's important to persist through the initial growing pains. One of the most effective ways to sustain action on a long-term goal is to chart incremental progress along the way. In his research on motivation and instruction, Stipek (1996) states that noting progress over time is a way of increasing personalization and persistence on a difficult task.

The rest of this chapter includes audit tools for teachers, students, and leaders to track the transformation process in the classroom.

So, as you begin to unlock your students' superpowers in the classroom, celebrate all the small wins along the way. Remember, all large-scale changes are derived from a series of additive, small shifts.

HOW SHOULD THESE AUDITS BE USED?

The audit tools presented in this chapter should be used as formative, not summative, tools. This means that the information generated by these tools should inform next steps, not to make an overall judgment about a teacher, a student, or a school's performance.

There are two main types of audits presented: a "Top Five Checklist" and an "Audit Rubric." Each has different uses and different goals.

The "Top Five Checklist" exists as a quick check that you can use either as a leader, teacher, or student to see if your planned activities are on track.

Conversely, the "Audit Rubric" can be used to provide in-depth feedback relative to a schoolwide initiative, unit, or lesson.

You can choose to use any combination of the tools that make sense to you in your specific situation. You may wish to make adjustments or amendments to these tools. If you create changes, use your professional judgment about the types of information and feedback that would be most helpful for students, teachers, and leaders.

Finally, every member of a learning community should be involved in auditing the classroom transformations suggested by this book. Have teachers provide peer feedback to each other. Have students share their opinions and voices at a forum, empowering the type of learning and authentic voice enabled by the student superpowers.

TOP FIVE CHECKLIST FOR TEACHERS

QUICK CHECK: HOW IS THIS UNIT SHAPING UP?

- ✓ Students have the opportunity to choose some/all of the topics explored during the learning experience.

✓ Students spend more time working/talking/sharing than the adult/teacher.

✓ Students find resources by themselves during the learning experience.

✓ Students have multiple opportunities to receive feedback on their work, either from self-reflection, peers, or the teacher.

✓ Students create a product for an authentic audience during the learning experience.

SUPERPOWER AUDIT RUBRIC FOR TEACHERS

IN-DEPTH REFLECTION: HOW IS MY CLASSROOM SHAPING UP?

OBSERVABLE	SUPERHERO	SIDEKICK	APPRENTICE
Student-Driven Topics	Students choose all (or almost all) of the topics for a given unit of study based on their individual interests.	Students choose some of the topics for a given unit of study based on their individual interests.	Teachers only focus units on established content topics.
Students Engaging in the Superpowers	Students engage in four to six of superpowers throughout the unit based on the learning goals. Students are able to articulate when they are engaging in the superpowers.	Students engage in one or two superpowers during the unit of study, but students cannot articulate when/how/why they are engaging in a superpower.	Students engage in a single superpower during the unit of study.
Access to Feedback	Students engage in self-reflection during the unit. Students have access to feedback from multiple sources that include peers, the teacher, and an authentic audience. Students actively seek out additional feedback when needed.	Students engage in some self-reflection. Students have access to one or two forms of feedback during the unit. Students are not yet confident seeking out additional feedback when needed.	Students receive feedback from the teacher during the unit.

TOP FIVE CHECKLIST FOR LEADERS

QUICK CHECK: HOW IS MY PLAN FOR THIS SCHOOL YEAR SHAPING UP?

✓ School policy supports curricular flexibility that allows students to choose some/all of the topics explored during a learning experience.

- ✓ Teachers are encouraged to invite authentic audiences into the classroom.
- ✓ Teachers have multiple, high-quality professional development opportunities to learn about new strategies or techniques.
- ✓ Teachers have multiple opportunities to receive feedback on their work, either from self-reflection, peers, or the teacher.
- ✓ Students have sufficient access to technology and training in the effective use of digital resources, allowing them to find information with increased independence.

GLOBAL SUPERPOWER AUDIT RUBRIC FOR LEADERS

IN-DEPTH REFLECTION: HOW IS MY SCHOOL/ORGANIZATION SHAPING UP?

OBSERVABLE	SUPERHERO	SIDEKICK	APPRENTICE
School Policies	School policies advocate for adjustments and changes to topical selections based on student interests. Most or all teachers feel empowered to implement such adjustments.	School policies generally support adjustments and changes to the curriculum. Some teachers feel safe in making these adjustments.	School policies advocate strict adherence to a pacing guide or curriculum calendar.
Access to Professional Development	Teachers have a variety of opportunities to experience professional development on topics that interest them. Both formal, on-site learning experiences and informal, independent learning experiences are valued.	Teachers have some opportunities to experience professional development on topics that interest them. Formal, conventional learning opportunities such as in-service days and workshops are valued in the school/organization.	Teachers have few opportunities to experience professional development on topics that interest them.
Access to Feedback	Teachers have the opportunity to receive feedback on their planning and instruction from both school leaders and peers on a regular basis. Common planning time is provided for teachers.	Teachers have a few opportunities to receive feedback on their instruction from school leaders and peers. This is more informal in nature, and time is not provided by the school/organization.	Teachers receive infrequent feedback from school leadership.

UNLEASHING STUDENT SUPERPOWERS

TOP FIVE CHECKLIST FOR STUDENTS

QUICK CHECK: HOW AM I DOING RIGHT NOW?

- ✓ Did I make good choices about my learning by selecting the topics that interest me most?

- ✓ Did I use time wisely during the learning experience today?

- ✓ Did I find good information that helps me learn about my topic?

- ✓ Did I make/create something that responds to the needs of my audience?

- ✓ Did I ask my peers, my teacher, and myself about the quality of my work?

SUPERPOWER AUDIT RUBRIC FOR STUDENTS

IN-DEPTH REFLECTION: HOW IS MY SCHOOL YEAR SHAPING UP?

OBSERVABLE	SUPERHERO	SIDEKICK	APPRENTICE
Self-Starting	I know what I am interested in and can easily decide what topics I need to explore to meet specific goals and create meaningful content. I am curious to learn about topics about which I know very little.	I can decide what topics I need to explore, but I sometimes need help from a teacher or a peer. I am curious, but often hesitant to investigate alone.	My teacher has to help me choose topics, and I have trouble figuring out where/how to begin. I want to make sure that I am doing work that the teacher wants.
Locating Resources	I can find everything I need to accomplish a goal. I use a variety of sources, including electronic resources, people, and text documents. I know how to figure out what is significant and connect it with other information.	I can find most things I need to accomplish a goal. Sometimes, peers or teachers let me know that I've missed an important resource for my work. I am working on figuring out what is important and what is not.	I need help from a teacher or a peer to find resources that relate to my topic. I often rely on only a few sources. I have trouble figuring out what is important and can waste time on resources that aren't.
Self-Monitoring	I reflect on my progress regularly. When working, I frequently consult peers, teachers, and experts in the field. I know when I need help to make my work better.	I reflect on my progress sometimes. When working, I consult peers and teachers frequently. I usually know when I need help to make my work better.	When working, I usually access feedback after a reminder from the teacher or a friend.

SUMMARY

The tools in this chapter are a starting point, not an ending point. Closely monitoring progress can be a fantastic way to motivate you and your students. Constant feedback is integral to improvement, and these tools can help you craft feedback that's actionable and effective.

• •

A QUESTION TO CONSIDER AS YOU REFLECT

- How can the need for continuous, honest feedback help to build better relationships with your colleagues and fellow school leaders? What specific mechanisms could be put in place to allow for and encourage these relationships? Make commitments.

START TODAY

TEN FIRST STEPS

FINDING SMALL WINS

As you reach the end of this book, you may be wondering: Where do I start? Some people like to start using the superpowers in their instruction by tackling an entire instructional journey. For others, a smaller start seems more appropriate. Consider these Ten First Steps as a way to begin the student superpower journey in your classroom. Remember, a series of small wins often sums up to a sizable change that impacts students!

1. IT'S ALL ABOUT CHOICE

The purpose of this strategy is to slowly empower students, most of whom expect to come into a classroom and be told what to do. By introducing It's All About Choice over a series of lessons, students increasingly learn how to take greater control of their learning.

To carry out this strategy,

1. Students choose specific aspects of a topic to be the focus of their investigation: one part of the cell; one explorer; one part of speech.

2. Students choose a specific outcome to show their learning: a poster; a piece of writing; a cartoon.

3. Students choose the type of homework that will help them recall the day's lesson: explain it to their parents; create a song; make a video.

4. Students choose broad topics of interest to investigate and share.

Related Superpowers and Frameworks: Wondering, Curating, Connecting, Digital Inking, Designing, Gaming

2. WHAT DOES GOOD WORK LOOK LIKE?

This strategy is an important part of empowering students as it allows them to regularly discuss personal goals. It helps them learn to challenge themselves, rather than simply trying to do whatever the teacher wants.

To carry out this strategy,

1. At the beginning of the school year, have students make a list of class standards. Avoid using the word *rules,* because that establishes the pattern that someone is going to be enforcing the rules. Pose the question: What does learning look like? This can be done first in small groups or as a class discussion. Avoid commenting on the student suggestions. Record them on the board. Have students choose their top ten.

2. At the beginning of each project or activity, establish project standards. What will a great project look like? What will excellent group work look like?

Related Superpowers and Frameworks: Wondering, Curating, Connecting, Digital Inking, Designing, Gaming

3. KNOWING WHAT I KNOW

This strategy helps students make meaning of their learning and growth. Students need to name the skills and superpowers that they are using and developing. As they learn to do this, the power in the classroom shifts away

from the teacher and toward the students. This is based on Peter Pappas'
work on developing a Reflective Student.

To carry out this strategy,

1. Start each day with the skills and superpowers clearly listed on the
    board. Have a student be responsible for reading them at the start
    of class. Students should make connections between the skills and
    superpowers of today and of past lessons, so that they are aware of
    how each lesson supports their learning.

2. On a regular basis, have the students write a reflection on their work,
    such as:

    -   What did I do well?

    -   What did I find challenging?

    -   What would I do differently if I had to do it again?

3. Collect the reflections. Study the needs and successes of each student
    to better prepare for the next lesson.

4. Keep the reflections. At the end of a unit, return them to the students
    as a means of sharing their growth.

Related Superpowers and Frameworks: Wondering, Curating,
Connecting, Digital Inking, Designing, Gaming

4. DIFFERENT EVERY DAY

This strategy engages students' curiosity and allows them to begin making
choices. Classrooms are often stagnant places where learning happens
in designated places and in specific ways. One of the ways to engage and
empower students is to change the classroom architecture on a regular
basis to help them see that learning happens in lots of different ways.

To carry out this strategy,

1. During each planning session, consider how to rearrange the
    classroom for the best learning environment. Make sure that change
    happens often. Discuss with the students why the furniture in the
    room changes.

2. Provide rugs, pillows. Create sections of the room, if possible.
    Allow students to choose where they want to be to accomplish their
    work.

3. Have students design their favorite way for a classroom to be designed. This could become a full Design Challenge or a single exercise. Test their ideas and have them receive feedback from other students.

Related Superpowers and Frameworks: Wondering, Curating, Connecting, Digital Inking, Designing, Gaming

5. LIST-GROUP-LABEL

This strategy is a great way to check students' thinking as well as refine their understanding of a complex topic. It is inductive in nature, which requires students to make meaning of their thoughts and specific content.

To carry out this strategy,

1. Have students create a list of all the possible responses to an open-ended prompt.
2. Have students group their responses into different categories that *they define*.
3. Have students define a brief label for each category.

Related Superpowers and Frameworks: Wondering, Curating, Connecting, Digital Inking

6. STUDENT-DIRECTED SHARE

This strategy helps students review what they've learned in a collaborative format. It only takes 5 minutes, and it allows students to have more control in the classroom. The strategy increases student ownership and choice in a small, manageable way.

To carry out this strategy,

1. Have students appoint one member of the class as the leader. (It's much more powerful if students do this, not you.)
2. Have students share one or two brief facts about what was learned in the previous class. (This can be done by passing a talking stick or simply having the appointed leader call on students.)

3. Allow the appointed student to summarize all comments at the end of the activity. (Use this as a segue or an introduction into the day's lesson, showing students that their work is building into something meaningful.)

Related Superpowers and Frameworks: Wondering, Curating, Connecting, Digital Inking, Designing, Gaming

7. THINK TIME

This strategy gives students time to develop their ideas. Often teachers ask for the answers to their questions immediately, allowing little space for thinking and developing new ideas. This strategy allows students time to do this, thus empowering them.

To carry out this strategy,

1. Discuss the role of Think Time with the students. Have them identify why it is important. Have them give an example of a time when they wished they'd thought of just the right thing to say at the right time.

2. Regularly provide Think Time, calling it by name. This can be done by establishing 10-second pauses after a question is asked or by having students write their response before they give it.

3. Take a Silent Walk after presenting a challenge or new task to allow students to generate their own ideas.

Related Superpowers and Frameworks: Wondering, Curating, Connecting, Digital Inking, Designing, Gaming

8. THREE-FINGER SELF-ASSESSMENT

The purpose of this strategy is to increase students' opportunities to evaluate their work. Self-assessment and metacognition are two of the most powerful methods for accelerating student achievement (Hattie, 2009).

To carry out this strategy,

1. Have students name a task that students have recently completed.

2. Ask students to evaluate their performance on the task using the three-finger strategy:

   - Students hold up three fingers if they felt they did a *great* job.
   - Students hold up two fingers if they felt they did an OK job.
   - Students hold up one finger if they are really confused and need more help on this task.

3. Celebrate student progress.

Related Superpowers and Frameworks: Wondering, Curating, Connecting, Digital Inking, Designing, Gaming

9. GALLERY WALK

A gallery walk can have two purposes. It can be a flexible method for sharing new content. Or, it can provide students with additional peer feedback on their work. In either case, students visit each station and leave comments in response to what they encounter. Comments can be guided by specific questions or a rubric if desired.

To carry out this strategy,

1. Have students work in groups and rotate between several different stations in the classroom that have a specific resource (student work sample, video, article, etc.).

2. Have students leave comments at each station relative to the resource. If the resource is a student work sample, students can leave feedback about the piece relative to a rubric. If the resource is a piece of new content, students can leave a reflection or reaction.

3. Hold a whole-group debrief to discuss common problems or opportunities spotted during the gallery walk.

Related Superpowers and Frameworks: Wondering, Curating, Connecting, Digital Inking, Designing, Gaming

10. A CLASS BLOG

Blogging with kids gives them access to authentic audiences. Kid bloggers often write prolifically and with engagement due to the interactivity of the medium. Writing digitally turns students into real authors!

To carry out this strategy,

1. Have students determine the types of topics that they'd like to explore on their blog.

2. Have students create a blog for the class. (Check out Kidblogs or Edublogs for details.)

3. Give students the opportunity to write and publish their thoughts on the class blog.

4. Share student work with parents and other stakeholders via social media and traditional communication channels such as Back to School Night.

5. Encourage everyone to leave comments and feedback on the student work samples.

6. Celebrate student success.

Related Superpowers and Frameworks: Connecting, Digital Inking

While these Ten First Steps will not completely transform your classroom, they can provide an effective way for you to get started. Everyone's learning journey is unique!

● ●

A QUESTION TO CONSIDER AS YOU REFLECT

- What First Steps can I implement *tomorrow* to give students more power in my classroom?

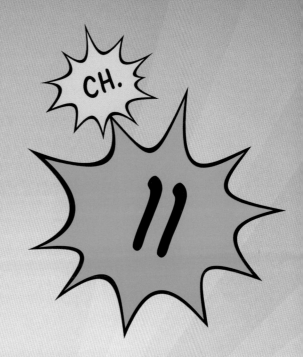

MORE READINGS

THE FAB FIVE

CONTINUING THE JOURNEY

If you've reached the end of this text and you're still hungry for more, don't fret! There are many related resources that you can explore to help you transform your instruction so that students develop the superpowers needed for life and work. The titles that follow are some of our favorite, practical explanations for the research, theories, and methodologies that inspired the creation of this text!

1. *MAKING LEARNING WHOLE* BY DAVID PERKINS

David Perkins, a member of Project Zero at Harvard, has closely studied the learning process for decades. This book is a fantastic, easy-to-understand summary of the research behind student-driven instruction. Through stories and examples, Perkins helps you prioritize the types of learning that are truly needed for today's ever-changing society.

2. *TEACHING THE iGENERATION* BY BILL FERRITER AND ADAM GARRY

Bill Ferriter is an amazing middle school teacher in North Carolina. His book focuses on creating the types of learning that students will need as technology changes the ways that we work, socialize, and grow. Organized around broad competencies such as managing information and telling stories, the ideas in the text will certainly outlast the specific technology tools cited within it!

3. *NET SMART* BY HOWARD RHINEGOLD AND ANTHONY WEEKS

Howard Rhinegold is considered to be one of the leading thinkers on how the Internet is shaping our world. In this text, you will learn about the need to intentionally harness our attention to ensure that the constant barrage of information and data does not harm us as people. The skills and research explored in this text have highly influenced many of the frameworks in this text, and they are critical to students' future success in college and career.

4. *MULTIPLIERS* BY LIZ WISEMAN AND GREG MCKEOWN

Although this book was written for business managers, the research foundation is tightly aligned with the student superpowers presented in this book. Wiseman and McKeown talk about the need to empower those around you, creating an environment that is conducive to both shared ownership and success! Giving students superpowers effectively creates the "multiplier effect" in an educational setting.

5. *HOW CHILDREN SUCCEED* BY PAUL TOUGH

In this text, Tough explores and shares the research behind grit, growth mindsets, and self-reflection. Using engaging stories and real-life examples, Tough makes the case that we need to view all learning as a formative journey. Tough uses research to assert that students who understand this will have better outcomes in life. Helping students to develop empowered selves that can overcome obstacles is one of the tenets for the frameworks in this book.

Consider this list a resource to help you deepen your understanding of the research and ideas that support a student-driven classroom.

● ●

A QUESTION TO CONSIDER AS YOU REFLECT

- What types of research or information can help me justify my practice to skeptical stakeholders such as parents, leaders, or board members?

REFERENCES

Australian Curriculum Studies Association, Inc. Australian Curriculum Studies Association, n.d. Web. 20 Aug. 2013. http://www.acsa.edu.au/pages/index.asp

Beecher, Henry Ward, n.d. Web. 22 Jan. 2014. http://www.goodreads.com/quotes/78685-we-should-not-judge-people-by-their-peak-of-excellence

d.school bootcamp bootleg. d.school, n.d. Web. 23 Jan. 2013. http://dschool.stanford.edu/wp-content/uploads/2011/03/BootcampBootleg2010v2SLIM.pdf

Ferriter, Bill, and Adam Garry. "Teaching Kids to Curate Content Collections." The Tempered Radical. Center for Teaching Quality, 14 Dec. 2012. Web. 19 Aug. 2013. http://blog.williamferriter.com/2012/12/14/curating-a-content-collection-activity

Gagne, Robert, and Richard White. "Memory Structures and Learning Outcomes." *Review of Educational Research* 48.2 (1978): 187–222.

Gardner, Howard. *Five Minds for the Future.* Boston: Harvard Business, 2008.

Hattie, John A. *Visible Learning.* New York City: Routledge, 2009.

IDEO Riverdale, ed. Design Thinking for Educators. IDEO, n.d. Web. 20 Aug. 2013. http://designthinkingforeducators.com

Koster, Ralph. *The Theory of Fun for Game Design.* Scottsdale: Paraglyph, 2005.

Lai, E. R. *Motivation: A Literature Review.* Pearson Research Report, 2011.

Leithauser, Brad. "The Box and the Keyhole." *New Yorker* 21 Nov. 2012: n. pag. *New Yorker.* Web. 20 Aug. 2013. http://www.newyorker.com/online/blogs/books/2012/11/the-box-and-the-keyhole-two-ways-of-looking-at-fiction.html#ixzz2DGZusr47

Lenhart, Amanda. "New Pew Internet/MacArthur Report on Teens, Video Games and Civics." Pew Internet (2008): n. pag. Pew Internet & American Life Project. Web. 20 Aug. 2013. http://www.pewinternet.org/Commentary/2008/September/New-Pew-InternetMacArthur-Report-on-Teens-Video-Games-and-Civics.aspx

Martinez, Sylvia Libow, and Gary Stager. *Invent to Learn.* Torrance: Constructing Modern Knowledge, 2013.

Marzano, R. J. *What Works in Schools: Translating Research into Action.* Alexandria: Association for Supervision & Curriculum Development, 2003.

National Council for the Social Studies. "The Themes of Social Studies." NCSS Website, 17 Sep. 2010. Web. 13 Nov. 2013. http://www.socialstudies.org/standards/strands

National Governors Association Center for Best Practices, Council of Chief State School Officers. *Common Core State Standards.* Washington, DC: National Governors Association Center for Best Practices, Council of Chief State School Officers, 2010.

National Research Council. *Education for Life and Work: Developing Transferable Knowledge and Skills in the 21st Century.* Washington, DC: National Academies, 2012.

Organization for Economic Cooperation and Development. Education at a Glance. OCED, 2002. Web, 20 Aug. 2013. http://www.oecd.org/edu/skills-beyond-school/educationataglance2002-home.htm

Perkins, David N. *Making Learning Whole: How Seven Principles of Teaching Can Transform Education.* Hoboken, NJ: John Wiley, 2012.

Pink, Daniel H. *A Whole New Mind.* New York City: Riverhead, 2006.

Prensky, Marc. *Teaching Digital Natives.* Thousand Oaks, CA: Corwin, 2010.

Rheingold, Howard, and Anthony Weeks. Net Smart. MIT Press, February 24, 2012.

Richardson, Will. Why School? How Education Must Change When Learning and Information Are Everywhere (Kindle Single) (Kindle Locations 65–67). TED Conferences, September 10, 2012.

Schmoker, Mike. *Focus: Elevating the Essentials to Radically Improve Student Learning.* Alexandria, VA: Association for Supervision & Curriculum Development, 2011.

Sprenger, Marilee. *Differentiation Through Learning Styles and Memory.* Thousand Oaks, CA: Corwin, 2003.

Stipek, D. Motivation and Instruction. In D. C. Berliner & R. C. Calfee. *Handbook of Educational Psychology.* (pp. 85–113). New York: Simon & Schuster, 1996.

Trilling, Bernie, and Charles Fadel. *21st Century Skills: Learning for Life in Our Times.* San Francisco: Jossey-Bass, 2009.

Tyler, Ralph. *Basic Principles of Curriculum and Instruction.* Chicago: University of Chicago, 2010.

Warlick, David. From yesterday's backchannel: "Uncertainty is not bad. 'When anything can happen, then anything is possible.'" 19 Feb. 2013, 2:37 p.m. Tweet. https://twitter.com/dwarlick/status/303815600105463811

Werbach, Kevin, and Dan Hunter. *Gamify for the Win.* Wharton Digital, 2012.

Wiggins, Grant. "Webinar on Design Thinking." Granted, and . . . Wordpress, 7 Mar. 2013. Web. 20 Aug. 2013. http://grantwiggins.wordpress.com/2013/03/07/webinar-on-design-thinking

Wiggins, Grant, and Jay McTighe. *Understanding by design* (2nd ed.). Alexandria, VA: Association for Supervision & Curriculum Development, 2005.

Wright, Steven. "Steven Wright > Quotes > Quotable Quote." *Goodreads, 2013.* Web. 21 Aug. 2013. http://www.goodreads.com/quotes/101936-there-was-a-power-outage-at-a-department-store-yesterday

INDEX

CORWIN

A SAGE Company

The Corwin logo—a raven striding across an open book—represents the union of courage and learning. Corwin is committed to improving education for all learners by publishing books and other professional development resources for those serving the field of PreK–12 education. By providing practical, hands-on materials, Corwin continues to carry out the promise of its motto: **"Helping Educators Do Their Work Better."**